Heroines

Heroines

The Lives of
GREAT LITERARY CHARACTERS
and What They Have to Teach Us

Mary Riso

Baker Books

A Division of Baker Book House Co
Grand Rapids, Michigan 49516

© 2003 by Mary Riso

Published by Baker Books
a division of Baker Book House Company
P.O. Box 6287, Grand Rapids, MI 49516-6287
www.bakerbooks.com

Printed in the United States of America

Library of Congress Cataloging-in-Publication Data
Heroines : the lives of great literary characters and what they have to teach us / [edited by] Mary Riso.
    p.   cm.
  ISBN 0-8010-6428-7 (pbk.)
    1. Women in literature. 2. Heroines in literature. 3. Fiction—20th century—History and criticism. 4. Fiction—19th century—History and criticism. I. Riso, Mary, 1960-
PN56.5.W64 R574 2003
809′.93352′042—dc21   2003000136

Scripture is taken from the Revised Standard Version of the Bible, copyright 1946, 1952, 1971 by the Division of Christian Education of the National Council of the Churches of Christ in the USA. Used by permission.

To my mother—Joan Riso

Whatever is true,
whatever is honorable,
whatever is just,
whatever is pure,
whatever is lovely,
whatever is gracious,
if there is any excellence,
if there is anything worthy of praise,
think about these things.

Philippians 4:8

Contents

Preface   9

1. The Lover   15

Natasha in *War and Peace*—L. N. Tolstoy   19
Jane in *Jane Eyre*—Charlotte Brontë   26
Lucy in The Chronicles of Narnia and the Green
   Lady in *Perelandra*—C. S. Lewis   33

2. The Keeper of Meaning   41

Anne in *Persuasion*—Jane Austen   48
Kitty in *Anna Karenin*—L. N. Tolstoy   56
Bobbie in *The Railway Children*—
   Edith Nesbit   64

3. The Woman of Courage   81

Elizabeth in *Pride and Prejudice*—
   Jane Austen   86
Betsey in *David Copperfield*—
   Charles Dickens   91
Pauline in *Descent into Hell*—
   Charles Williams   101

4. The Wise Woman   117

Psyche in *Till We Have Faces*—C. S. Lewis   121
Celia in *The Cocktail Party*—T. S. Eliot   128
Julia in *Brideshead Revisited*—
    Evelyn Waugh   137

5. The Ennobler   153

Mary in *The Secret Garden*—
    Frances Hodgson Burnett   157
Alice in *Can You Forgive Her?*—
    Anthony Trollope   168
Lucie in *A Tale of Two Cities*—
    Charles Dickens   173

Epilogue   185
Notes   188
Recommended Video Versions of
    Selected Titles   192

Preface

"You will never tell your father this," the low, beautiful voice went on; "you must not even tell your sister until you have rescued Dickie and made the sacrifice. This is the one supreme chance of all your life. Every soul has one such chance, a chance to be perfectly unselfish, absolutely noble and true. You can take this chance. But you must take it alone. No one can help you. No one can advise you. And you must keep the nobler thought in your own heart till it is a noble deed. Then, humbly and thankfully in that you have been permitted to do so fine and brave a thing and to draw near to the immortals of all ages who have such deeds to do and have done them, then you may tell the truth to the one who loves you best, your sister Elfrida."

"But isn't Elfrida to have a chance to be noble too?" Edred asked.

"She will have a thousand chances to be good and noble. And she will take them all. But she will never know that she has done it."

Edith Nesbit[1]

When I was a child I often visited the library near our home. The building was originally a family home, a mansion complete with a winding staircase, fireplaces, enormous sofas and leather chairs, polished wood floors—and of course, thousands of books from floor to ceiling. One of the things I loved best was to pretend I was the lady of the mansion and wander from room to room, imagining myself graceful, wise, good, and beautiful. Through this act of pretending I made a step toward acquiring some of these qualities, just as I did when I read books about the heroines who possessed them or struggled for them.

When I was eight years old my mother and I went to a store called Toy Town in Bronxville, New York, and left with a beautifully illustrated copy of *The Secret Garden* by Frances Hodgson Burnett. Today, when I gently lay aside the tattered book jacket, I am reminded of the day I first entered the world of Mary Lennox. Mary is an orphan who discovers a dead garden and restores it to life, awakening her own life in the process and restoring hope and truth to another child who is convinced he is going to die. I took one look at this book and instantly fell in love with it. As I watched Mary search for the garden until she found it and loved it, and wander the halls of Misselthwaite Manor following a boy's cry, I saw that she was unique and knew that I was too. She was stubborn and intelligent and interested in people. I wondered if I could be like her.

I was first introduced to C. S. Lewis's Chronicles of Narnia by my brother after his fourth grade teacher read *The Silver Chair* aloud to the class. Lucy quickly became my favorite character. Appearing in five of the seven titles in the series, Lucy had courage, honesty, a generous and kind spirit, affection, discernment, peace of mind, and the capacity to enjoy life. However, I rarely thought of these things as I read of her adventures. I knew that she had a special relationship with Aslan (God), and I loved that about her. I knew that I could rely on her to do what I hoped I would do in the same situation. I was fairly certain that we might be afraid of the same things and like the same things. Lucy found Narnia first, saw Aslan most often, and did not seem to think about herself very much. I wondered if I was anything like her, or could be if I tried.

The next year my parents gave me *Little Women* by Louisa May Alcott for Christmas. Of course I could not put it down. What little girl has not wanted to be Jo? She is a complicated heroine, and while there are certainly characteristics worthy of imitation, there are also those worthy of being left behind. The theme of loss in Jo's life can seem overwhelming for a child who has known loss. I cried through the second half of the book. Even then I half knew that what mattered was Jo's response to her sufferings. Was there hope in the midst of despair? If there was I could embrace it and store it away. If not, then I would instinctively turn away from it. Recently I reread this with a friend in Italy, discussing it via e-mail, and we marveled at the reality of Meg, Jo, Beth, and Amy. We felt we knew them and related to them, caring not only about their decisions but wondering about the motivation of the author. I suddenly realized the remarkable capacity of this novel to draw the reader into its world. I also realized the underlying melancholy, reflecting the pain and disappointments of the author's life. I cried at the same places, but now I knew why. God used it as a channel to release some of my own pain. All this was accomplished through imaginary characters in a work of fiction.

The books mentioned thus far were written for children, although they are treasures for all ages. As the years went on I met Jane Austen; Charlotte, Emily, and Anne Brontë; George MacDonald; Charles Dickens; J. R. R. Tolkien; Edith Nesbit; Victor Hugo; and L. N. Tolstoy, among others. There are many reasons to read their works. However, in keeping with the theme of this book, here are three observations.

First, the *facts*. Fiction is full of wonderful boys and girls, men and women. The great heroes and heroines of fiction display certain characteristics, many of which are shared by both sexes. However, we are particularly concerned here with feminine giftedness. The fact is that there *is* such giftedness. The question is: What gifts contribute to the makeup of a heroine? There are so many! However, in this book you will find some of your favorite friends of literature grouped into five expressions of the "true feminine"[2]: the lover, the keeper of meaning, the woman of courage, the wise woman, and the ennobler. There is also the "false feminine," and many characters possess both the false and the true, doing battle until the true feminine is victorious. When this is so, it is possible that the author was engaged in the same battle. The importance of discernment cannot be overemphasized—the false and the true should be recognized for what they are. These scenarios can be invaluable to the reader in learning to practice objectivity and discerning truth from falsehood.

Another fact is that the writer of fiction has a responsibility to the reader. People may disagree as to the nature of this responsibility, but I believe that, if the author knows God, it is to call the reader out of the limits of the self to grow into a soul indwelled by God. This is a high calling. The authors touched upon in this book have made an attempt to fulfill this calling. Many of them have looked deep into their hearts and found the heart of God. They have drawn upon the objective and solid reality of God-given virtues and placed these virtues in the fruit of their imagination—the characters in their books.

This is an incredible gift to share with others. The *fruit* of the author's imagination produces fruit in the heart of the reader. It is also an enormous responsibility, since the reader absorbs the fruit of the author's imagination unconsciously and also with an awareness of what may be gained. Unfortunately, if the author loves evil, then evil will be communicated. If the author loves good, then good will be communicated. In cases where the imagination of the author has been sanctified by the Holy Spirit, the reader can be exposed to new vistas of God's creation and hopes for the human soul. And when the imagination of both author and reader are prepared by the Spirit of God, great fruit may be produced, resulting in the growth of the reader's soul. That is why it is so important for the author to write with a consciousness of responsibility and for the reader to choose material carefully.

Part of what readers do when they open a work of fiction is to choose what role models they want to *follow*. This is a genuine responsibility for the reader if he or she wants to go "further in and higher up"[3] in the Christian life. There are books that nurture the soul, whether or not such was the author's explicit intention. It is important to know that there are heroes and heroines, role models for both children and adults, in fiction as well as nonfiction. It is a wonderful goal to seek these heroes out and share their lives, to know both the authors and their work. It is also possible to imitate what is good and true and to practice being what you want to be but are not yet.

Know the *facts*, eat the *fruits*, and *follow* the truth. Good fiction replete with a true heroine and real virtue draws the reader to its ultimate source—the Creator of all things.

Just as I walked through that beautiful library, I hope that whoever reads this book will enjoy walking a little way with some of the heroines of literature. These char-

acters can shed a light on that piece of our hearts, perhaps hidden or buried, perhaps yet unborn, that God
longs to bring to life. An encounter with them can initiate a longing to be more than we are and all that we
can be in Christ, our hope of glory.

1

The Lover

Neither did she consider that it was not seemly, and that it looked ill, to go and weep and shed tears among the guests, provided that, without delaying an hour or waiting for another time and season, she could reach Him for love of Whom her soul was already wounded and enkindled. And such is the inebriating power and the boldness of love, that, though she knew her Beloved to be enclosed in the sepulchre by the great sealed stone, and surrounded by soldiers who were guarding Him lest His disciples should steal Him away, she allowed none of these things to impede her, but went before daybreak with the ointments to anoint Him.

St. John of the Cross[1]

One of the things we look for in fictional characters, if we wish to imitate them, is someone who truly knows how to love. However, love is an overused and often misunderstood word. God asks for obedience, responsiveness, and trust, and these qualities are what Jesus searches for in His followers. Jesus also makes it clear that obedience and love are inseparable: "If a man loves me, he will keep my word, and my Father will love him, and we will come to him and make our home with him" (John 14:23).

God, our Creator, nurtures and protects us and is described as a rock, a fortress, our shield, and our defender. We can trust Him to take care of us.

> See that you do not despise one of these little ones; for I tell you that in heaven their angels always behold the face of my Father who is in heaven. What do you think? If a man has a hundred sheep, and one of them has gone astray, does he not leave the ninety-nine on the Mountains and go in search of the one that went astray? And if he finds it, truly, I say to you, he rejoices over it more than over the ninety-nine that never went astray. So it is not the will of my Father who is in heaven that one of these little ones should perish.
>
> Matthew 18:10–14

Another aspect of love is sacrifice—imitating Christ in His willingness to lay down His life for others. (This is not to be confused with substitution—attempting to literally take on the sin or suffering of another human being, something only Jesus can do.) One of the most powerful statements Jesus made about love is found in the Gospel of John: "Greater love has no man than this, that a man lay down his life for his friends" (John 15:13).

These aspects of love are to be experienced by men and women alike. In the words of Alice von Hildebrand, professor emeritus of the City University of New York: "There are no male knees and female knees—all knees on heaven and earth should kneel to Jesus—adoration is the only proper response to Him for everyone."[2] More than half of the authors covered in this book are men; both men and women understand what contributes to true heroism. Men may not understand women from the inside out, but they do have the advantage of objectivity and often see things that elude women.

Here we are looking primarily at heroines of literature. We will see how women act out virtue in a particular way that is true to their nature. Just as there are
obvious differences between male and female, so masculine and feminine represent different things. A modern understanding of these differences tends to incor-
porate more of the "false masculine" and the "false
feminine," which emphasize aggression and passivity
respectively. However, the true manifestations of the
masculine and feminine found in initiation and response
are not only present in our relationships with one
another, or in works of art such as those we will look at,
but first in the relationship between God and His children, between Christ and the church.

In C. S. Lewis's *The Voyage of the Dawn Treader:* "Then
[Lucy's] face lit up till, for a moment (but of course she
didn't know it), she looked almost as beautiful as that
other Lucy in the picture, and she ran forward with a
little cry of delight and with her arms stretched out. For
what stood in the doorway was Aslan Himself, the Lion,
the highest of all High Kings. And He was solid and real
and warm and He let her kiss and bury herself in His
shining mane."[3] The dominating feature in this scene is
that Lucy is in the presence of Love with a capital "L"—
that Love is a person—and not a feeling or an action of
human proportions. An attitude of trusting response is
a key part of what it means to be feminine, and when a
man experiences this he is in touch with the true feminine within himself. A woman has a similar experience,
but it is likely that she has different qualities that need
to be strengthened.

> Elisabeth Elliot . . . states that "the essence of mas-
> culinity is initiation and the essence of femininity is
> response." For a woman to be free to initiate—free, that
> is, to hear the word of the Lord and do what she hears

Him say—is for her to be in touch with the true masculine aspect. She is not sickly passive—the feminine principle estranged from the masculine. She is free to respond to God with all her being, and therefore able to *initiate* when the occasion calls for it. In the upright, vertical relationship to her Lord, she is fully a person, fully enabled to collaborate with His Spirit. She is a balanced feminine *maker* in the image of her Creator Father.

. . . [An] imbalance of the power to initiate and the power to respond can always be healed when a person forsakes his *vision and will in separation from God* (what the Scripture calls dying to the old man), comes into the Presence, and there unites with the incredible realities outside himself.[4]

There is a sense in which the true masculine and the true feminine compliment each other in a healthy human soul, but with a different emphasis depending on whether one is male or female. Ultimately, however, love is about relationship. Even if God had never created the world and all the living things in it, love would have existed within the Trinity. The many aspects of love—obedience, trust, responsiveness, protection, and sacrifice—often shine the brightest in situations with eternal consequences. When life is lived in faith everything has eternal consequences, including the most commonplace activities and daily encounters. Throughout the Scriptures and continuing through history to the present day are countless examples of women loving against the light of the supernatural. In literature and other works of art we see evidence of the same objective reality.

Natasha *in War and Peace*

L. N. Tolstoy

Generosity, Inner Beauty, and Sacrifice

We would recognize her in a thousand, Natasha Rostov, "not pretty, black-eyed, with a wide, expressive mouth . . . narrow shoulders, bare arms full of childish grace." . . . Everyone, at some point, draws near to her, is lit up by and glows in her flame. "Whatever she did, she threw herself into it, body and soul," wrote Tolstoy.[5]

At the heart of Tolstoy's (1828–1910) *War and Peace* is Natasha: genuine, charming, and imperfect. It is a delight to live in her presence for almost two thousand pages. It would perhaps be less delightful if she had no weaknesses, no terrible choices to make, nothing to invite the reader into her heart from the great distance that at first divides fiction from reality. In his own notes about her Tolstoy wrote, "Prodigal . . . Self-confident . . . Loved by all . . . Proud . . . Musical."[6] When I first encountered Natasha I had the overwhelming impression that her soul found a direct path to her eyes without any detours or stop signs. It rested there, shining, throughout the entire book. I could see the tremendous capacity to love, the forgiveness given and received, the selfishness, and the generosity. The most precious aspect of her character was her generous and open heart—to give and to receive. When she did wrong she had the capacity to see it and to say the three most important words in the world: "I am sorry." Observing her joyful and loving nature made me realize my own self-imposed limitations and self-protectiveness. Reading her story made me see anew the redemptive power of forgiveness.

Natasha is described as "not beautiful." Yet everyone who has read *War and Peace* knows that Natasha Rostov is beautiful. This is because her inner life and outer life become increasingly integrated and her soul illuminates her physical being. She reminds me of a woman I knew in college who was not physically attractive in the conventional sense. Yet some of the most wonderful men on campus were in love with her. I saw in her an authenticity and complete lack of self-consciousness that were irresistible. In *War and Peace* Natasha struggles to choose what is right and does not always succeed. Yet she has a soft heart and a sensitive conscience to the voice of truth. By listening to this voice she changes, blessing others with the image of her true self.

> "Forgive me!" she said in a whisper, lifting her head and glancing at him. "Forgive me!"
>
> "I love you," said Prince Andrei.
>
> "Forgive . . ."
>
> "Forgive what?" he asked.
>
> "Forgive me for what I di-d!" faltered Natasha in a scarcely audible, broken whisper, and again began quickly covering his hand with kisses, softly brushing her lips against it.
>
> "I love you more, better than before," said Prince Andrei, raising her face with his hand so as to look into her eyes.
>
> Those eyes, swimming with happy tears, gazed at him with timid commiseration and joyous love. Natasha's

thin, white face with its swollen lips was more than plain—it looked ghastly. But Prince Andrei did not see her face, he saw the shining eyes which were beautiful.[7]

"It is only against the light of the supernatural that we can truly discover the unique privilege of being a woman."[8] Sometimes true love is found like a gem sparkling in the fire of suffering and repentance. When the thin, invisible veil that rests between this life and eternity is temporarily lifted for those who stand in the presence of imminent death, the light of the supernatural can shine on the most dreadful circumstances, burning and changing the face of love with all of its immature devotion to self and emotion until a pure and indestructible diamond of self-giving remains, a reflection of the love of Christ on the cross.

This happens for both Natasha and Prince Andrei as they stand on the brink of Andrei's entrance into eternity. The above passage, however, appears almost three-quarters of the way through Tolstoy's masterpiece. In the approximately eleven hundred pages prior to this, Natasha shows many of the faces of love as she grows from a girl of thirteen to a young woman of twenty. She is Tolstoy's idealized vision of young girlhood, and yet she has a breathtaking reality as well that defies the author's limitations and instead reflects his God-given genius for portraying eternity in a moment and ageless joy in a glimpse of a sixteen-year-old girl. "And yet, after all, the clock is not always ticking. Sometimes it stops and then we are happiest. Sometimes—more precisely, some-not-times—we find 'the still point of the turning world'. All our most lovely moments perhaps are timeless."[9]

"Sonya! Sonya!" said the first voice again. "Oh, how can you sleep? Just look how lovely it is! Oh, how glorious!

Do wake up, Sonya!" and there were almost tears in the voice. "There never, never was such an exquisite night."

Sonya made some reluctant reply.

"No, but do look what a moon! . . . Oh, how lovely! Do come here. Darling, precious, come here! There, you see? I feel like squatting down on my heels, putting my arms around my knees like this, tight—tight as can be—and flying away! Like this . . ."

"Take care or you'll fall out."

He heard the sound of a scuffle and Sonya's disapproving voice. "Why, it's past one o'clock."

"Oh, you only spoil things for me. All right, go to bed then, go along!"

Again all was silent, but Prince Andrei knew she was still sitting there. From time to time he heard a soft rustle or a sigh.

"O God, O God, what does it mean?" she exclaimed suddenly. "To bed then, if I must!" and she slammed the casement. . . .

All at once such an unexpected turmoil of youthful thoughts and hopes, contrary to the whole tenor of his life, surged up in his heart that, feeling incapable of explaining his condition to himself, he made haste to lie down and fall asleep.[10]

The impression one receives in this passage is that there is an intensity of life and a capacity to love in this girl that overflows onto everything around her: the night, the moon, the very air she is breathing. She wants to break free of her physical limitations and soar into the sky, to get closer to the beauty she sees. There is something incomprehensible about it all, something that cannot be grasped ("O God, what does it mean?"). One could almost say she is in love with the moon, with herself, with the creation, with life—and she wants a place to put that love. There is a sense of frustration because there is no receptacle for her soul's worth.

Natasha's passionate, spontaneous nature and deep capacity to love are captivating and draw her into relationships that cause her bliss and pain, but these aspects of her nature also give the reader a glimpse of eternity every time she appears. There is a place in eternity for such love, and there is a place in the human soul for such love. Prince Andrei feels it and longs for it the first time he sets eyes on her, without fully knowing what it is he feels and longs for. He does not yet recognize his own capacity to love. Indeed, neither Prince Andrei nor Natasha know what love is when they meet and fall in love at her first ball.

> Like all men who have grown up in society, Prince Andrei enjoyed meeting someone not of the conventional society stamp. And such was Natasha, with her wonder, her delight, her shyness and even her mistakes in speaking French. His manner was particularly tender and careful. As he sat beside her talking of the simplest and most insignificant matters, he admired the radiance of her eyes and her smile which had to do with her own inner happiness and not with what they were saying. . . .
>
> Natasha had never been so happy. She was at that highest pitch of bliss when one becomes completely good and kind, and cannot believe in the existence or possibility of evil, unhappiness and sorrow.[11]

It is only later, through sin and repentance, suffering and rejection, and the approach of death that they are blessed with the miracle of experiencing true love in its most perfect state.

> "Human love may turn to hatred but divine love cannot change. Nothing, not even death, can destroy it. It is the very nature of the soul. Yet how many people have I hated in my life? And of them all none did I love and

hate as much as her. . . . If only I might see her once more. Just once to look into those eyes and say . . ."[12]

In between her first and last meeting with Prince Andrei, the face of Natasha's love changes several times. As all of her powers of devotion focus on one man, she seems stunned and bewildered, hardly understanding what it is she is experiencing. It is a combination of an immature infatuation with Andrei, with love itself, and with a sincere womanly decision to marry this man. At times Natasha seems to be all emotion and intuition with little reasoning power or objective vision. She is young—only about seventeen—at this time, and it is this combination of youth and reliance on the extreme subjective feminine that leads to her near seduction by another man. Andrei, in pride and rejection, refuses to forgive her for this, and the sin of both lies between them despite their genuine love for each other.

When they meet again they have separately experienced terrible suffering of the spirit and the body. They have seen beyond the surface of their lives and are consciously aware of the potential for love and for sin within themselves and each other. They have acknowledged their sin and now long only to receive forgiveness and live in love. This capacity to love is discovered only in the context of their relationship with all of its disappointment and pain. Natasha's spiritual awakening follows the loss of Prince Andrei, and the loss of her pride and self-respect. Prince Andrei's spiritual awakening follows his confrontation with death and the awareness of his own sin. Rightly related to God, they can be rightly related to one another at last. The reality of their own spiritual state makes a love possible that defies youth, pride, and time and only grows stronger in the face of death. They are ready to sacrifice for each other instead of putting their own feelings and needs first.

When love for another human being is involved, there is always the danger that the lovers may seek to find their identity in one another rather than in God. This is especially dangerous for a woman, for whom relationship is so important. However, the primary relationship for any man or woman must be with God. Only our Creator can tell us who we are, and it is a terrible mistake to crave a sense of worth or identity from any other human being. If we do not look up to God to answer the questions Who am I? and Why am I here? we will surely turn to a human relationship with those questions in tow, for they must be answered.

Jane in *Jane Eyre*
Charlotte Brontë

Loyalty to Objective Reality

Conventionality is not morality. Self-righteousness is not religion. To attack the first is not to assail the last. To pluck the mask from the face of the Pharisee, is not to lift an impious hand to the Crown of Thorns. These things and deeds are diametrically opposed: they are as distinct as vice is from virtue. Men too often confound them: they should not be confounded; appearance should not be mistaken for truth; narrow human doctrines, that only tend to elate and magnify a few, should not be substituted for the world-redeeming word of Christ.

Charlotte Brontë[13]

One of the strongest pictures in all classic literature of one who was deprived of a stable home environment and affectionate parents is found in the title character of Charlotte Brontë's (1816–1855) *Jane Eyre*. Jane is an orphan from infancy, brought up in an atmosphere of pervasive evil—first in the home of an aunt who hates her and then from the age of ten in a boarding school run by a mentally disturbed headmaster, who seems to do everything in his power to destroy the children in his care both spiritually and physically.

Surely if any young girl would be disposed to turn to a fellow creature not only for love and nurturing but for a sense of worth and identity it is Jane. At eighteen she leaves the school to begin employment as a governess in the home of a wealthy and mysterious man. When she and that man fall in love with each other, it would hardly be surprising if she were to lose herself in him and be completely submissive, relieved to have found someone to love her at last. And yet such is not the case. Jane's belief in God and the knowledge of right and wrong that she has received from Him are the basis for her life and decisions. This is doubly surprising because both her aunt and the headmaster used God as an excuse for their evil behavior and certainly gave Jane every good reason to turn from Him. However, as she grows to love her employer, Mr. Rochester, she never places him above God; indeed, her response to him appears to be coming from her upright position toward God.

This consistency in her relationship with God does not diminish her youth, lack of sophistication, or love for her employer; she is in love with him and her need of him does blind her to his nature to some degree. However, she is not controlled by him. This is particularly striking because, in their most prominent works *(Jane Eyre, Wuthering Heights,* and *The Tenant of Wildfell Hall),* all three of the Brontë sisters tended to portray their primary male characters as bitter and brooding, if not brutal. With some authors of the same period there was also a tendency to create passive female characters. *Jane Eyre* has plenty of this fallen masculine image, but Jane's character is noticeably forthright, decisive, and self-protective rather than destructive. In conversation her head is clear; she knows what she thinks and expresses herself well with little apparent regard for the opinion of

Mr. Rochester. In moments of temptation she does not turn from the narrow way, despite the enormous temptation to do so.

For many years I felt that in loving this story and its heroine as much as I did I was doing something wrong. This was because I recognized the presence of the false masculine in Rochester and a battle with the false feminine in Jane's relationship with him. As a Christian I felt it might be damaging to "practice the presence" of these things in the course of my reading. However, I slowly came to an understanding based on God's wisdom rather than my own fears.

First, I saw that my anxiety with regard to this work and other Victorian literature was based partly on my fear that I was not completely free from the false or passive feminine myself, nor fully separated from the false masculine. It is true that the male/female relationships in these works can be attractive to the reader for the wrong reasons, feeding a desire or need to live out of the false self. It is important to read each book with an eye to discerning truth from falsehood and an open heart to recognize a victory in the life of a character and be inspired by it. While it is true that some authors of the Victorian period communicate more of their own cynicism and despair than anything else, for others redemption and hope is the final word.

Second, the genuine Christian content of much Victorian literature is often underestimated or misunderstood because it is assumed to be purely nominal, the result of a self-satisfied culture, or reduced to an absurd evangelical stereotype obviously disapproved of by the author and all right-thinking people. A careful reading of many works of that period exposes this superficial interpretation. *Jane Eyre* is a particularly good example of this because the powerful spiritual content is encased in a fascinating and at times disturbing love story cast in a bleak setting. When the following conversations between Jane and Rochester are gathered together, however, it is impossible not to see Jane's real belief and Rochester's journey to repentance.

"I wish I had stood firm—God knows I do! Dread remorse when you are tempted to err, Miss Eyre: remorse is the poison of life."

"Repentance is said to be its cure, sir."

"It is not its cure. Reformation may be its cure; and I could reform—I have strength yet for that—if—but where is the use of thinking of it, hampered, burdened, cursed as I am? Besides, since happiness is irrevocably denied me, I have a right to get pleasure out of life: and I *will* get it, cost what it may."

"Then you will degenerate still more, sir."

"Possibly: yet why should I, if I can get sweet, fresh pleasure? And I may get it as sweet and fresh as the wild honey the bee gathers on the moor."

"It will sting—it will taste bitter, sir."[14]

"I see no enemy to a fortunate issue but in the brow; and that brow professes to say—'I can live alone, if self-respect and circumstances require me to do so. I need not sell my soul to buy bliss. I have an inward treasure born with me, which can keep me alive if all extraneous delights should be withheld, or offered only at a price I cannot afford to give. . . . Strong wind, earthquake shock, and fire may pass by: but I shall follow the guiding of that still small voice which interprets the dictates of conscience.'"[15]

"I like to serve you, sir, and to obey you in all that is right."

"Precisely: I see you do . . . for if I bid you to do what you thought wrong . . . my friend would then turn to me, quiet and pale, and would say, 'No sir; that is impossible: I cannot do it, because it is wrong'; and would become as immutable as a fixed star."[16]

"Is the wandering and sinful, but now rest-seeking and repentant, man justified in daring the world's opinion, in order to attach to him for ever to this gentle, gracious, genial stranger, thereby securing his own peace of mind and regeneration of life?"

"Sir," I answered, "a wanderer's repose or a sinner's reformation should never depend on a fellow creature. Men and women die; philosophers falter in wisdom, and Christians in goodness; if anyone you know has suffered and erred, let him look higher than his equals for strength to amend and solace to heal."[17]

"What shall I do, Jane? Where turn for a companion, and for some hope?"

"Do as I do: trust in God and yourself. Believe in Heaven. Hope to meet there again."

"Then you will not yield?"

"No."

"Then you condemn me to live wretched and die accursed?" His voice rose.

"I advise you to live sinless and to die tranquil."

Still indomitable was the reply: "*I* care for myself. The more solitary, the more friendless, the more unsustained I am, the more I will respect myself. I will keep the law given by God; sanctioned by man. I will hold to the principles received by me when I was sane, and not mad—as I am now. Laws and principles are not for times when there is no temptation; they are for such moments as this, when body and soul rise in mutiny against their rigour; stringent are they; inviolate they shall be. If at my individual convenience I might break them, what would be their worth?"[18]

"Jane! you think me, I dare say, an irreligious dog: but my heart swells with gratitude to the beneficent God of this earth just now. He sees not as man sees, but far clearer: judges not as man judges, but far more wisely. I did wrong: I would have sullied my innocent flower— breathed guilt on its purity: the Omnipotent snatched it from me. I, in my stiff-necked rebellion, almost cursed the dispensation: instead of bending to the decree, I defied it. Divine justice pursued its course; disasters came thick on me: I was forced to pass through the valley of the shadow of death. . . . Of late, Jane—only— only of late—I began to see and acknowledge the hand of God in my doom. I began to experience remorse, repentance, the wish for reconcilement to my Maker. I began sometimes to pray: very brief prayers they were, but very sincere."[19]

Jane's love of God, her willingness to obey His commands even while suffering, and her belief in His promises take precedence over her devotion to her intended husband. Her love for God is acted out in obedience and her need for the love of a man is not victorious over her conscience and the witness of the Holy Spirit. Her perspective, sense of humor, and honesty are never corrupted by a series of wrong choices, as are the same qualities in Mr. Rochester. Ultimately both Jane and Rochester are transformed by a love for one another that can only be truly fulfilled when both have placed God on the throne of their hearts.

Jane is a heroine worthy of imitation, not despite her struggles but because of them. She possesses a rare combination of emotional vulnerability and a solid loyalty to objective truth. It is this that makes her so appealing as a friend, governess, and wife. Not only is she loyal to God, who is her truest friend; she has courage and perseverance as well. Her identity is not as an eternal orphan, but as a child of God who is able in turn to love the abandoned child, Adele, who is placed in her care.

As a child Jane knew the truth (and to hear her speak it is wonderful) but sought to respond to it with vengeance.

> "I am glad you are no relation of mine. I will never call you aunt again as long as I live. I will never come to see you when I am grown up; and if anyone asks me how I liked you, and how you treated me, I will say the very thought of you makes me sick, and that you treated me with miserable cruelty."
> "How dare you affirm that, Jane Eyre?"
> "How dare I, Mrs. Reed? How dare I? Because it is the *truth*."[20]

Later, she is able to forgive her aunt and to ask forgiveness as well. As a woman with no worldly possessions, she has enough inner resources to forgive those who hated and abused her.

> "Dear Mrs. Reed," said I, . . . "think no more of all this, let it pass away from your mind. Forgive me for my passionate language; I was a child then; eight, nine years have passed since that day. . . . Love me, then, or hate me, as you will. . . . You have my full and free forgiveness: ask now for God's and be at peace."[21]

Starting out in the world with no home, no money, and no friends, Jane finds her true home with God and takes that with her. Alone in the world, she knows she is never alone and is able to make the choices she does based on that knowledge. If her soul were desolate she would surely have gone with Mr. Rochester instead of into the wilderness. In the end, her loyalty to God is vindicated and bears fruit not only in her own life but in the life of the man she loves.

Lucy in *The Chronicles of Narnia* and *The Green Lady* in *Perelandra*

C. S. Lewis

Trust and Obedience

Certainly C. S. Lewis (1898–1963) had a remarkable gift for portraying God as One who is at once majestic and accessible, King and Father, Creator and Suffering Servant. He shows how God can and must be as precious and longed for to us as a most beloved spouse, child, mother, brother, or friend. I began reading Lewis's Chronicles of Narnia when I was nine. When I was seventeen, during a period of rejecting the faith of my childhood, I remember saying that I could more easily believe in and relate to Aslan than I could to Jesus. For some reason I could not yet see that one was a symbol of the other. (About eighteen months later I returned to Christ while reading *The Great Divorce* by the same author.) The most wonderful scenes in the Chronicles are those in which Aslan is central. Lewis lifts up Christ in such a way that all are drawn to Him. God has made us to want Him and to love Him; He is not foreign to us.

33

When Lucy meets Aslan again in *Prince Caspian* after a period of separation, she responds out of a complete integration of mind, heart, soul, and body. This happy scene is reminiscent of the responses of Mary Magdalene, Peter, John, and others when Jesus appeared to them after His resurrection.

> A circle of grass, smooth as a lawn, met her eyes, with dark trees dancing all round it. And—oh joy! For *he* was there: the huge Lion, shining white in the moonlight with his huge black shadow underneath him.
>
> But for the movement of his tail he might have been a stone lion, but Lucy never thought of that. She never stopped to think whether he was a friendly lion or not. She rushed to him. She felt her heart would burst if she lost a moment. And the next thing she knew was that she was kissing him and putting her arms as far round his neck as she could and burying her face in the beautiful rich silkiness of his mane.
>
> "Aslan, Aslan. Dear Aslan," sobbed Lucy. "At last."[22]

One of the loveliest expressions of the masculine/feminine balance is the word of Aslan to Lucy in *The Voyage of the Dawn Treader* when in the moment of her extreme fear he whispers to her, "Courage, dear heart,"[23] imparting the masculine and cherishing the feminine. It is not the only time he breathes strength and courage into her.

> "It is hard for you, little one," said Aslan. . . .
>
> Lucy buried her head in his mane to hide from his face. But there must have been magic in his mane. She could feel lion-strength go into her. Quite suddenly she sat up.
>
> "I'm sorry, Aslan," she said. "I'm ready now."
>
> "Now you are a lioness," said Aslan. "And now all Narnia will be renewed."[24]

Lucy is brave and a true follower of Aslan, as is evidenced by her name: Queen Lucy the Valiant. Responsiveness is not passivity. She fights in the wars and heals those who are hurt. In this balance, as in the names Lucy the Valiant and her sister Susan the Gentle, is a clear picture of the true feminine. This balance is the key to the feminine nature and to the nature of love.

In *Perelandra,* the second volume in C. S. Lewis's science fiction trilogy, we see an attempt to destroy that attitude of trust and self-forgetfulness that comes from focusing on God with love as Lucy does, and in so doing to throw off the natural balance between Creator and creature. In the words of the Green Lady:

> "I think He made one law of that kind in order that there might be obedience. In all these other matters what you call obeying Him is but doing what seems good in your own eyes also. Is love content with that? You do them, indeed, because they are His will, but not only because they are His will. Where can you taste the joy of obeying unless He bids you do something for which His bidding is the *only* reason?"[25]

It is said that men have the capacity to "compartmentalize"—to separate intellect and body and emotions—more easily than women. This is probably true, although many women have developed a greater capacity for this in a world where it is increasingly important to "hold it all together": career and family and loyalty to God and church. How else can one do this if not by organizing one's life into neat compartments, *doing* more and *being* less. But this is particularly dangerous for a woman because any such system will inevitably subordinate the heart to the head, causing a division between them. And when a woman is cut off from her

heart, from the intuitive feeling part of herself, she sacrifices her special giftedness.

That is why it is also particularly devastating emo-
tionally for a woman to engage in a promiscuous
lifestyle, although it is certainly equally dangerous for
both men and women on a spiritual level. A woman does
not separate her body from her emotions and her emotions from her intellect. A physical relationship with a
man involves more than just her body. A woman who
has many intimate relationships is literally giving her
whole self away again and again until the grief over that
loss and the loss of her lovers is all but inconsolable.

The integration of head and heart, and the perfect
obedience that grows out of perfect trust, is beautifully
illustrated in C. S. Lewis's *Perelandra*. Here, the Lady,
the perfect woman, the Eve of the planet Venus, has
never had any sense of observing herself as if she could
separate herself into pieces or become two people—
until she meets men from earth, one of whom gives her
a mirror.

> "Things being two when they are one," replied the Lady
> decisively. "That thing" (she pointed at the mirror) "is
> me and not me."
>
> "But if you do not look you will never know how beau-
> tiful you are."
>
> "It comes into my mind, Stranger," she answered,
> "that a fruit does not eat itself, and a man cannot be
> altogether with himself." . . . Ransom perceived that the
> affair of the robes and the mirror had been only super-
> ficially concerned with what is commonly called female
> vanity. The image of her beautiful body had been offered
> to her only as a means to awake the far more perilous
> image of her great soul. The external, and, as it were,
> dramatic conception of the self was the enemy's true
> aim. He was making her mind a theatre in which that
> phantom self should hold the stage.[26]

The enemy wants to introduce self-consciousness to this new Eve—and with it fear and pride and self-concern. Up to this point self-consciousness was foreign to her. She not only knew no separation from herself; she knew no separation from Maleldil (Jesus); she belongs to Him and it is inconceivable for her to do anything but love and obey Him. Love and obedience are inseparable—they are her true response to Maleldil, as should be true for us all. Love is ideally an integrated experience for men *and* women. It is the body running to embrace Him, the joy of the heart at the sight of Him, the worship of the heart in gratitude. However, there is no need to investigate our own responses so closely. In our relationship with Him who lives within us, it is better to lose the consciousness of self as much as possible.

> "I begin to wonder," said the Lady after a pause, "whether you are so much older than I. Surely what you are saying is like a fruit with no taste! How can I step out of His will save into something that cannot be wished? Shall I start trying not to love Him—or the King—or the beasts? It would be like trying to walk on water or swim through islands. Shall I try not to sleep or to drink or to laugh? I thought your words had a meaning. But now it seems they have none. To walk out of His will is to walk into nowhere."[27]

> The word *Lady* had made no part of his vocabulary save as pure form or else in mockery. He had laughed too soon.[28]

Concluding Comments

The paintings of Rembrandt, Rubens, Correggio, and many others show kings, animals, and shepherds gazing at a newborn Jesus with undisguised wonder and longing. We read in 2 Corinthians 5:21: "For our sake he made him to be sin who knew no sin, so that in him we might become the righteousness of God." Suddenly we are back to the basics. We realize that the lives of countless Christians through the ages attest to a deep gratitude and love at the sight of the cross. There is the sense that if we do not know what it is to adore the Savior we have missed the point of life.

All love on the part of human beings is a response to God. It is a response to Someone who has given His life for you; it is a response because this same One has given us the capacity to love. Without Him we would be utterly incapable of experiencing love; indeed, we would cease to be.

> In this is love, not that we loved God but that he loved us and sent his Son to be the expiation for our sins. Beloved, if God so loved us, we also ought to love one another. No one has ever seen God; but if we love one another, God abides in us and his love is perfected in us.
>
> 1 John 4:10–12

There is a sense, particularly in human relationships, in which love is a choice, a decision of the will and not simply a feeling. Nowhere is this clearer than in 1 Corinthians 13. Certainly if anything is a choice, it is to be patient and kind, to not be jealous, boastful, arrogant, or rude. But how would such choices even be possible for sinful human beings without the author of love writing these options on our hearts and in the universe? Love of God for both men and women is therefore essentially feminine in nature; it is a response to His love and to His initiative. In the words of C. S. Lewis, "What is above and beyond all things is so masculine that we are all feminine in relation to it."[29] There is only one uncreated Being and everything else exists in relationship to Him: "in him we live and move and have our being" (Acts 17:28).

It is of vital importance to the wholeness of a woman's soul to allow this God-given love to flow freely and not stifle it, horde it, or fear the expenditure of it. That letting go, receiving "God's love [that] has been poured into our hearts through the Holy Spirit" (Rom. 5:5) and allowing the "living waters" promised by Jesus to flow forth unhindered is the key to all that that love inspires: passion, tenderness, courage, loyalty, obedience, trust, whole-hearted devotion, and joy. Because the love comes to us from the source of love it can never run out or be used up. And it should never be used as a bargaining tool; it is a free gift.

If carefully chosen, fictional characters, the creation of God's creation, can prove to be excellent role models for learning how to love.

Prayer

If you then, who are evil, know how to give good gifts to your children, how much more will the heavenly Father give the Holy Spirit to those who ask him!

Luke 11:13

Dear Father,

Thank You for the gift of Your Holy Spirit, for I know that Your life in me is all I need to become the woman You want me to be. Please bring beautiful fruit from that precious gift.

I especially ask that You would pour Your love into my heart in such abundance that it may overflow to those around me. I ask that when others look at me they would see Your radiant love shining from my soul. Let inner beauty be my goal.

Help me to be as trusting and obedient as Your Son, Jesus; help me to respond to You in love as did His mother, Mary.

Give me the wisdom and discernment to choose good books to read and good role models to follow.

Give me the grace and strength to always be loyal to and love the truth that is You.

Restore to me true femininity, and heal entirely anything false that is the result of my own sins and the sins of others.

Most of all, open my heart to receive Your love and a vision of You as You truly are. May I find my true self in You and no one else, and live in Your presence day and night.

In the name of Your Son, Jesus,
Amen

2

The Keeper of Meaning

"Is there, do you think, anything seriously very wrong with me?"
"There is nothing wrong with you," said Miss Ironwood.
"You mean it will go away?"
"I have no means of telling. I should say probably not."
"Then—can't anything be done about it? They were horrible dreams—horribly vivid, not like dreams at all."
"I can quite understand that."
"Is it something that can't be cured?"
"The reason you cannot be cured is that you are not ill."

C. S. Lewis[1]

In approaching the topic of this section I am inspired by the words of Oswald Chambers: "Always make a practice of stirring up your own mind to think out what it accepts easily."[2] This is an attempt to capture in words a subtle and often silent experience. Unlike the Lover, whose action often precedes feeling and whose obedience may lead to bold action, the Keeper of Meaning makes observations and preserves objective truth, both in the most commonplace and the most dramatic of circumstances. There is nothing subtle or ethereal about the Lover of the world dying on the cross. However, that same Keeper of Meaning saw and understood the heart of every soul He encountered and often spoke but few words.

If love is a waterfall pouring from the heart of God, then imbedded in that waterfall is a rough yet precious gem, primal, living, submerged, but always poised to connect with the world above the water. This is transcendent meaning: the meaning hidden in all of reality because of the divine life that is its source. In the words of George MacDonald, "In the Lord we find the perfecting of all the dull hints of precious things which common humanity affords to us."[3]

The phrase "life is meaningless" is untrue; indeed, there is far too much meaning for the human heart to hold unless that heart is the home of God. I was reminded of this on September 11, 2001, when, after the initial attack on the World Trade Center and before the buildings collapsed, I watched on television as thousands of pieces of paper—memos and letters from lawyers, brokers, secretaries, and CEOs—fluttered through the air and soon covered sidewalks. Later that day I was disturbed to hear someone say that this was symbolic of the futility of capitalism and the brevity and uncertainty of life on earth. My reaction was quite different. That poignant sight convinced me of the importance of every human soul where the mind and hands collaborated to write a letter to another human soul. Never was I so overwhelmed by the importance of human life than at that moment. Those pieces of paper had too much meaning, not too little. Truly, there is more to be seen than meets the eye. As Lucy says in the last book in The Chronicles of Narnia, "a Stable once had something inside it that was bigger than our whole world."[4]

Meaning may be kept in the heart on many levels. On one level, it is an awareness of truth on a grand scale: at times a sharp, bright awareness like a candle flame leaping to life in a light breeze; at others, a slightly bewildered insight into someone's heart, even the heart of God. It is knowledge of what matters, despite appearances, and confidence in this knowledge. The Keeper of Meaning takes the pattern of the universe for granted and attaches this pattern to life's encounters. This is often accomplished unintentionally; a perception of infinite meaning does not necessarily include the ability to define it with precision. It is often kept silently and with little introspection or even full comprehension. Only God can refine it with delicate use and the infusion of wisdom.

In human relationships the Keeper of Meaning is very alert, and the closer the relationship the more remarkable the intuition into the true self, named and called by God. It is not wisdom or discernment but rather an ability to perceive the meaning in action, expression, or word and sometimes to reflect that meaning back to the person with or without words. The Keeper of Meaning looks outward and is unconcerned with self. The intuition of meaning is directed toward others and the world. The simplest of settings can set the stage for an intuition of meaning, as we shall see in the lives of Kitty, Anne, and Bobbie. However, when a person understands and accepts a simple fact about a life outside herself—something dear to the heart of that life—and does not seek to alter that fact according to a personal agenda, it is powerful and important.

Women as Keepers of Meaning are found frequently in literature. While not the exclusive province of women, this might be called a special province, particularly when manifested in the context of human relationship. Although based on a strong, almost thoughtless trust of the inner heart, the observations of the Keeper of Meaning are supremely objective in that their content is not opinion but fact. However, intuiting meaning does not have to do with understanding. Rather, it has to do with knowledge. One can know something is true without understanding it.

Being a Keeper of Meaning can range from knowledge of a person's character to receiving insight into events on a worldwide scale to perceiving a cultural shift in the colors of a child's coat.

> The essence, the very core of true culture is beauty. And I'm sorry to say that for the last fifty years we seem to have been extremely untalented at producing things that are truly beautiful and we are extraordinarily talented at producing ugliness. . . . Plato said that it is so important that a child should be taught what beauty is from the moment that he is born and exposed to it so that by the time he is mature he will instinctively see—this is good, and this is evil. This is to be accepted and this is to be rejected. In a society that creates ugliness, not only in architecture and toys—but in our clothing, we teach children to enjoy looking at things that have bad proportions or ugly colors. For example, the coats of young children today have twelve different colors: there is no harmony, no proportion, no unity, no beauty. . . . This is true because there is no receptivity.[5]

Alice von Hildebrand speaks here of receptivity to God in our capacity as creators of beauty. We can only create beauty when we receive from Him who is the author of beauty. When women can no longer receive rightly from God they have lost a large part of the true feminine.

The following is a dream recounted by the character of Georgina in the British television series, *Upstairs*

Downstairs, on the brink of World War I. Georgina is about twenty years old at the time and has no conscious knowledge of the terrible evil that is about to destroy so many of her generation. However, in her dream she has a glimpse into what lies ahead; bewildered and disturbed by it, she shares the dream with her maid.

> I was on a swing in a big park somewhere, and there was a young man sitting beside me, tall and rather good-looking. . . . Down below there were masses of people, all cheering and waving flags at us. Oh, and then I saw the young man's face. It was dreadfully white, as if all the blood had been drained away. And then suddenly he just fell off the swing miles and miles below to the ground. And I wanted to go down there to help him in case he wasn't dead. But then I saw that by falling he'd somehow managed to knock down every one of the people who were waving flags and cheering. And they were all young men too, with the same white, drained faces. And some of them were bleeding and crying out.[6]

In all of these cases the mere fact that meaning exists matters enormously. Literature is important because it shows us that somewhere sometime someone understood what was really there—not what she wanted to be there. Someone cared about a matter of little interest to her because someone she loved cared about it; someone had a dream that extended beyond her own individual life and wondered what it meant; someone cared about the color of a child's coat and with God's help put meaning into words.

The Keeper of Meaning has a gift that carries a responsibility. To be a Keeper of Meaning requires a commitment to God that allows Him to refine that rough gem, giving it structure that one may share with others. Then one may act with wisdom when acting at all from the storehouse of meaning. Here the feminine needs the masculine to give expression to meaning, and the two work in complementary fashion, as they often do. However, one of the characteristics of this sort of knowledge is that it rests in the heart; it is possible that it may never be shared with others. It just *is*. The Keeper of Meaning has the capacity to *be* in the presence of God without constant activity. Meaning has to do with what is important and true on the level of the soul and in the world from God's point of view. Keeping this meaning requires imitation of Him and submission to His will, for the meaning is kept in the heart where He dwells. A perfect example of this is Mary, who, after hearing of the message brought to the shepherds by the angels, "kept all these things, pondering them in her heart" (Luke 2:19). God always knows the content of the heart, and whether truth is verbalized or not, it is kept for eternity.

Where is the virtue in this? One cannot help intuiting reality. Josef Pieper, in his book *A Brief Reader on the Virtues of the Human Heart,* speaks of the virtue of prudence, which is the classic virtue closest to keeping meaning. The prudent person "does not allow his view on reality to be controlled by the Yes or No of his will, but rather makes this Yes or No of the will dependent upon the truth of real things."[7]

> Even the highest supernatural prudence can have no other meaning than this: to allow the more deeply experienced truth of the reality of God and of the world to become the measure and standard for one's own desire and action. Indeed, never can there be a norm for man other than Being itself as well as Truth, whereby Being is revealed; and there can be no higher norm for man than simply God, who simply is, along with his truth.[8]

To live responsibly towards God and man one must imitate the greatest Keeper of Meaning who ever lived—

Jesus (different in that He not only saw but always understood what He saw). "In doing righteously, in loving mercy, in walking humbly, the conviction increased that Jesus knew the very secret of human life."[9] Ideally, the Keeper of Meaning

- is comfortable with silence and chooses words carefully
- is outward-looking and not self-conscious
- has the capacity to be and yet is not passive
- trusts her heart and listens for the voice of God
- asks the Father for wisdom
- accepts the responsibility God has given and uses it under God's direction
- is humble towards God and others
- finds her identity in God alone and consents to being misunderstood at times

This may seem like a tall order, but the imitation of Christ is the imitation of perfection. To be like Him is our destiny as Christians, but it is a process that takes place over a lifetime and into eternity. An enormous advantage, and a way that we can cooperate in the process of sanctification, is reading books that nurture the soul, with characters worthy of admiration and imitation. They can also help us to see dangers that may lie ahead. The three women in this chapter may help to shed light on a place within, largely ignored and little understood, which in the hands of God may be anointed to gently touch lives for others. For those women (and men) who see truth and are bewildered, these characters may help them to understand how God works in the soul. For those who see truth and wonder if they are alone, there is reassurance in these works of literature that they are in good company.

Anne in Persuasion

Jane Austen

The Importance of Individual Choice

> She was a humble, believing Christian. . . . I do not venture to speak of her religious principle: that is a subject on which she herself was more inclined to *think* and *act* than to *talk*, and I shall imitate her reserve, satisfied to have shown how much of Christian love and humility abounded in her heart, without promising to lay bare the roots whence those graces grew.
>
> J. E. Austen-Leigh[10]

All of Jane Austen's (1775–1817) heroines seem to reflect one or more aspects of the author's character: In Lizzy of *Pride and Prejudice* we see her humor and sense of perspective; in Elinor of *Sense and Sensibility* and Fanny of *Mansfield Park* is the ability to keep intense feeling under control and put duty before need; in the title character of *Emma* are the strengths that could easily become weaknesses without humility; in Catherine of *Northanger Abbey* we see the difference between real feeling and maudlin sentimentality, her distaste for the melodramatic romance novel, so different from her own objective and subtle style (indeed, she claimed that she "could not sit seriously down to write a serious romance under any motive than to save my life"[11]). In all of them is the ability to take an interest in life and other people despite personal disappointment.

And then there is Anne of *Persuasion*. The first charming thing about Anne Elliot is that such a thoughtful, principled, and intelligent woman is also so vulnerable. The second is that she is an excellent judge of character without being unkind. And the third is that she never lies to herself. In all of these respects, and especially in the first, she holds something within that is true and that is partially hidden from the world—this is what makes her a Keeper of Meaning.

Throughout the book she displays the combination of strength and vulnerability that are the hallmarks of true femininity. Anne exhibits certain characteristics that further reflect the true feminine—she is sensitive but not hypersensitive; she expresses true feeling but is not petulant or gossipy; she is self-aware but has no self-pity or self-hatred; she is underappreciated by those around her but does not dwell on the fact and hardly seems aware of it. In contrast, there is at least one female character who represents aspects of the false feminine rejected by Anne. Anne's sister Mary seems to have embraced the false feminine with all her strength and stubbornness and consequently is an unappealing character whose narcissism makes her miserable and pushes others away.

Relative to other literary figures of the nineteenth century, we know little about Jane Austen. But it can safely be said that she was a woman of deep feeling, often contained by the greatest good sense, and that she was a keen observer of humanity, but without a hint of cruelty in her conclusions.

There were differing opinions about Jane Austen's work during her lifetime; to this day some regard it as superficial and conventional (although in the last ten years she has received a great deal of attention and renewed regard through the film versions of her books).

Her contemporaries appeared to either love or hate her books. One of the many who loved them was Sir Walter Scott, who wrote in his diary on March 14, 1826:

> Read again, for the third time at least, Miss Austen's finely written novel of "Pride and Prejudice." The young lady had a talent for describing the involvements and feelings and characters of ordinary life, which is to me the most wonderful I ever met with. The big Bow-Wow strain I can do myself like any now going; but the exquisite touch which renders ordinary common-place things and characters interesting from the truth of the description and the sentiment is denied to me.[12]

It is indeed in character study and in the immense importance of the individual and individual choices that Jane Austen shines. Eight years before *Persuasion* begins Anne Elliot made a choice. She rejected the man she loved and who loved her because she was persuaded to do so, based on his lack of prospects, by a trusted friend. The story is about how this man, Captain Wentworth, reenters Anne's life and how hope is gradually revived for both. Anne must go through the process of allowing the rebirth of this hope, and it is here that she must accept the invitation to be vulnerable.

Her need to give and to receive love is great. Anne knows this about herself, and from the moment of Captain Wentworth's reappearance, she cannot lie to herself about it. Few people recognize this about Anne for she is very self-contained and those around her are remarkably self-absorbed. Admiral and Mrs. Croft, Wentworth's sister and brother-in-law, sensitive people themselves, seem to see into her heart, and her invalid friend, Mrs. Smith, sees her as a separate individual. However, Anne is not valued by her nearest relations and is often underestimated by acquaintances. Nonetheless, even after years of heartbreak and regret when her sense of self has suffered, she knows that her choices are still important. Indeed, she knows this now better than she did eight years earlier.

Although the situation is different in that the love between Anne and Wentworth is mutual, one is reminded of Jo March, the heroine of *Little Women*. Several years after rejecting Laurie's proposal she comments: "I *am* lonely, and perhaps if Teddy had tried again I might have said 'Yes,' not because I love him any more, but because I care more to be loved than when he went away."[13] It is not easy for some women to admit the need for the love of a man. It is perhaps particularly difficult for Anne who lives at a time when her age of twenty-seven is the equivalent of forty-seven today. Yet for women vulnerability and the ability to receive are as important as other types of strength. As Anne receives the attentions of her cousin, Mr. Elliot, and also allows herself to acknowledge that Captain Wentworth still cares for her, she is physically transformed. The change is so apparent that several people, including her father and her friend Lady Russell, comment on how pretty she is becoming—as opposed to her "vanished bloom" at the opening of the story, which even Captain Wentworth noticed, much to Anne's hurt. She was "so altered he should not have known [her] again."[14]

Anne comes into full bloom as hope and love revive in her life, and it is true that people in general look their best when they know they are loved. That is why it is so important to see others, as much as possible, through the eyes of God. The truth or falsehood reflected in the eyes is meaningful. It is touching to watch as Anne slowly allows herself to believe the unbelievable. She is being given the chance to redeem her mistake. What matters now is not her ultimate choice should Wentworth offer again; she knows her answer will be "Yes." What matters is her (and his) choice to be open to love and to risk being hurt again.

In two lovely scenes we see how much Anne and Wentworth *matter* to each other. Since we experience things from Anne's perspective we see the importance of this man to her and the power for good or evil (in these cases for good) of the smallest gesture. At this point Anne is still very fragile, not daring to hope that Wentworth still loves her but certainly not denying her own intense feelings for a moment. Both are instances of care and protection on Wentworth's part towards Anne, who is clearly unused to this kind of treatment since she has no husband or brothers and has a father and sisters who largely neglect her. In the first scene, Wentworth helps her with her toddler nephew, Walter:

> In another moment, however, she found herself in the state of being released from him; someone was taking him from her, though he had bent down her head so much, that his little sturdy hands were unfastened from around her neck, and he was resolutely borne away, before she knew that Captain Wentworth had done it.
>
> Her sensations on the discovery made her perfectly speechless. She could not even thank him. She could only hang over little Charles, with the most disordered feelings. His kindness in stepping forward to her relief—the manner—the silence in which it had passed—the little particulars of the circumstance—with the conviction soon forced on her by the noise he was studiously making with the child, that he meant to avoid hearing her thanks.[15]

In the second scene, Wentworth sees that Anne is tired during a long walk and takes action:

> Yes,—he had done it. She was in the carriage, and felt that he had placed her there, that his will and his hands had done it, that she owed it to his perception of her fatigue, and his resolution to give her rest. She was very much affected by the view of his disposition towards her which all these things made apparent. This little circumstance seemed the completion of all that had gone before. She understood him. He could not forgive her,— but he could not be unfeeling. Though condemning her for the past, and considering it with high and unjust resentment, though perfectly careless of her, and though becoming attached to another, still he could not see her suffer, without the desire of giving her relief. It was a remainder of former sentiment; it was an impulse of pure, though unacknowledged friendship; it was a proof of his own warm and amiable heart, which she could not contemplate without emotions so compounded of pleasure and pain, that she knew not which prevailed.[16]

It is a tribute to the genius of the author that in reading these passages we perceive the meaning of these seemingly small actions through Anne's eyes, and thus they take on the meaning they truly deserve. Once again, it cannot be stressed enough that these choices of Wentworth's matter enormously, that the individual soul matters for all eternity. Jane Austen brings our attention to the obvious, to what we are thinking, to what matters, often *telling* in addition to *showing*—and it is so delightful that she does.

Two more scenes illustrate the hope that is now shining in full strength in the hearts of both Anne and Wentworth. On a rainy day in Bath . . .

> She now felt a great inclination to go to the outer door; she wanted to see if it rained. Why was she to suspect

herself of another motive? . . . She was sent back, however, in a moment by the entrance of Captain Wentworth
himself. . . . He was more obviously struck and confused
by the sight of her, than she had ever observed before;
he looked quite red. For the first time, since their
renewed acquaintance, she felt that she was betraying
the least sensibility of the two. She had the advantage
of him, in the preparation of the last few moments. All
the overpowering, blinding, bewildering, first effects of
strong surprise were over with her. Still, however, she
had enough to feel! It was agitation, pain, pleasure, a
something between delight and misery.[17]

And, finally, at a concert in the same city . . .

His choice of subjects, his expressions, and still more
his manner and look, had been such as she could see in
only one light. His opinion of Louisa Musgrove's inferi-
ority, an opinion which he had seemed solicitous to give,
his wonder at Captain Benwick, his feelings as to a first,
strong attachment,—sentences began which he could
not finish—his half averted eyes, and more than half
expressive glance,—all, all declared that he had a heart
returning to her at least; that anger, resentment, avoid-
ance, were no more; and that they were succeeded, not
merely by friendship and regard, but by the tenderness
of the past; yes, some share of the tenderness of the past.
She could not contemplate the change as implying
less.—He must love her.[18]

Hope is important. Choice is important. But one must
choose to hope. One must choose to be vulnerable, to
love, to treat others well, to be honest with oneself, with
others, with God. When Anne rejected Captain Wentworth she could never have guessed at the suffering that
choice would cause. Her choice affected not only herself but others, including Wentworth, other women he

considered marrying, and the men who loved those women. Wentworth also chose to allow pride to stand in the way of renewing his offer two years after Anne's initial refusal. However, the wonderful thing about living in a world created by a loving God is that our wrong choices may be redeemed. In *Persuasion* Anne and Wentworth have the opportunity to find each other again in this world. Other choices have repercussions that seem more permanent. But even these remain under God's mercy, as is so beautifully illustrated in this passage from "Babette's Feast" by Isak Dinesen:

> Man, my friends, is frail and foolish. We have all been told that grace is to be found in the universe. But in our human foolishness and short-sightedness we imagine divine grace to be finite. . . . We tremble before making our choice in life, and after having made it again tremble in fear of having chosen wrong. But the moment comes when our eyes are opened, and we see and realize that grace is infinite. . . . See! That which we have chosen is given us, and that which we have refused is, also and at the same time, granted us. Aye, that which we rejected is poured upon us abundantly. For mercy and truth have met together, and righteousness and bliss have kissed one another![19]

Anne's and Wentworth's sufferings are not meaningless, for God used those eight years to form character, and that character produces the hope that is needed when the time comes for a new choice to be made.

> We rejoice in our sufferings, knowing that suffering produces endurance, and endurance produces character, and character produces hope, and hope does not disappoint us, because God's love has been poured into our hearts through the Holy Spirit which has been given to us.
>
> Romans 5:3–5

Kitty in *Anna Karenin*
L. N. Tolstoy

> *"This Treasure in Earthen Vessels"*

And just as the conclusions of the astronomers would have been idle and precarious had they not been founded on observations of the visible heavens in relation to a single meridian and a single horizon, so all my conclusions would be idle and precarious if not founded on that understanding of good and evil which was and always will be alike for all men, which has been revealed to me by Christianity and which can always be trusted in my own soul . . .

"Oh, you haven't gone in yet?" he suddenly heard Kitty's voice, as she passed that way to the drawing room. "You're not upset about anything, are you?" she inquired, peering intently into his face in the starlight.

But she would not have been able to make out its expression had not a flash of lightning that blotted out the stars illuminated it for her. The lightning showed her his face distinctly, and seeing that he was calm and happy she smiled at him.

"She understands," he thought. "She knows what I am thinking about. Shall I tell her or not? Yes, I will . . ." But just as he opened his mouth to speak she turned to him first.

"Oh, Kostya, be nice and go and see if Sergei Ivanich will be comfortable in the corner room . . ."

"Very well, I'll go directly," said Levin, straightening up and kissing her.

"No, I had better not speak of it," he thought, as she passed in before him. "It is a secret for me alone, of vital importance for me, and not to be put into words."

L. N. Tolstoy[20]

Kitty, the youngest daughter of the Scherbatsky family and the wife of Levin in Tolstoy's *Anna Karenin* believes that she has a soul, that God exists, and that life is meaningful. These assumptions, common in nineteenth-century Russia, are in sharp contrast to today when even professing Christians sometimes behave like materialists, as if the soul, which cannot be perceived by the five senses, does not exist. The faith of one such as Kitty—childlike yet bearing mature fruit and able to glimpse the hidden regions beyond the thin curtain that stands between this life and the next—this faith, so foundational to Russian culture, was a target of the hatred and evil of communism. The Western world has also embraced materialism, but for other reasons, and this culture has affected even believing Christians who are disintegrated within to the point where intellect rules over heart instead of the two functioning together. Christians have lost the gift of reason and have also forgotten how to trust their own hearts wherein God dwells.

Kitty is not one of these. Unlike her husband who arrives at belief after a long and agonizing search, Kitty instinctively knows her place in God's world and, assuming that everyone else has a soul, believes that they all have a purpose and value as well. "It was a characteristic of Kitty's always to expect to find all the most excellent qualities in people, especially in those who were strangers to her."[21] She keeps meaning, quite simply, because she believes in God; this faith encourages her to see the best in strangers, to have insight into acquaintances, and to have an uncanny understanding of those she loves. Her clear, truthful eyes, which are remarked upon continually throughout the novel, are windows to her own soul, to her "subtle, complex inner life"; they are also windows *from* her soul to others. She is an ambassador for Christ without realizing it, communicating the truth of Christianity, including the meaning it gives to life. Her faith *is* instinctive; she grew up with it, and it was part of the air she breathed.

Still, she goes through a process of rediscovery. At one point she doubts her belief. Disappointed in herself and others, and projecting this onto God, she attempts to forsake her natural, spontaneous belief and takes her spiritual temperature, evaluating her piety. Her conscious motives for this are good, but the result is, in Kitty, false. "Kitty, for a time, sees no value in her lifestyle, longs to reject the selfishness of her past, and follow a route which seems to provide her with answers and a purpose. The arrival of her father, however, a truthful man who is very much at home with himself, seems to reflect back to her the falseness of her position."[22]

Kitty embodies the healthy feminine on many levels. She is able to receive truth on the level of both heart and reason; these two are not in conflict. She marries a man who will treat her with kindness and respect; she is outspoken but not petulant (although the combination of her spontaneity and youth and immaturity can sometimes lead her to say hurtful things to those she loves, such as her sister Dolly and her friend Varenka); she is capable of strong emotion but not maudlin sentiment. She is often inspired by love and compassion, and she has insights into mysteries that puzzle her intellectual husband and insights into his character—a character that often baffles others. She is aware that she is attractive to men, but this only spills over into vanity when she is very young and in a superficial way. Levin is in love with her: she is sweet and pretty, but he is drawn to much more than that.

> Serene and thoughtful, full of a subtle, complex inner life, remote from Levin, she was gazing beyond him at the glow of the sunrise.
>
> At the very instant when this vision was vanishing, the candid eyes fell on him. She recognized him, and a look of wonder and delight lit up her face.
>
> He could not be mistaken. There were no other eyes like those in the world. There was only one creature in the world that could concentrate for him all the light and meaning of life. It was she. It was Kitty.
>
> "No," he said to himself, "however good that simple life of toil may be, I cannot go back to it. I love *her*."[23]

There is no question that Levin sees transcendent meaning in the eyes, in the voice, in the being of the one he loves. "He had nothing especial to say to her but he longed to hear the sound of her voice . . . listening more to the sound of her voice than to the words she was saying."[24] And Kitty, for her part, sees the same in her husband. She has a remarkable ability to perceive her husband's meaning, even when he cannot express it or does not know it. "She had completely caught and found the right words for his badly expressed idea. Levin gave a smile of pleasure: he was so struck by the transition from the confused, verbose discussion with his brother and Pestsov to this laconic, clear, almost wordless communication of a very complex idea."[25] His smallest expression communicates to her, and this is because "her husband's soul was dearer [to her] than anything in the world."[26]

Here, keeping meaning is not so far removed from love. "She told him that she loved him because she understood him perfectly, because she knew what he would like, and everything he liked was good."[27] Despite his torment over his longing for God and struggle to believe that permeates the whole book, Kitty sees the latent faith in his soul that does bloom in the end. "She was religious and had never doubted the truths of religion, but his external unbelief did not affect her in the least. Through her love she knew his whole soul, and in his soul saw what she wanted; and the fact that his spiritual condition was called agnosticism troubled her not at all."[28] Kitty believes that without faith there can be no salvation and no eternal life for her husband; she simply cannot believe in Levin's professions of agnosticism. They seem unreal to her based on the evidence of her eyes and heart. She knows her husband is seeking and is miserable without God.

> "Why does he keep on reading those philosophy books of his all the year round?" she wondered. "If it's all written in those books, he can understand them. If what they say is all wrong, why read them? He says himself that he would like to believe. Then why doesn't he? It must be because he thinks too much. . . . He an unbeliever indeed! With his heart, his dread of hurting anyone's feelings, even a child's! With him it's everything for others, nothing for himself."[29]

As can be seen in the opening quote to this section, Levin does find God—or is found by Him—in the end.

Not only does Kitty perceive meaning in her husband on this deep level, but in other ways they are attuned to each other, as in this delightful conversation about the possible marriage of Levin's brother and Kitty's friend.

"Yes, but now with Varenka . . . I fancy there's something . . ."

"Perhaps there is. . . . But one has to know him. . . .
He's a peculiar, wonderful person. He's bound up in the
spiritual life. He's a man of too pure, too exalted a
nature."

"What, you mean this would lower him?"

"No, but he's so used to living a purely spiritual life
that he can't reconcile himself with actual fact, and
Varenka is, after all, fact."

Levin had grown used by now to uttering his thought
boldly, without taking the trouble to clothe it in exact
language; he knew that his wife, in such moments of loving tenderness as now, from a hint would understand
what he meant to say, and she did understand him . . .

"I envy him because he is better than I am . . . and
that's why he can be serene and contented."

"And you?" Kitty asked with a mocking, affectionate
smile.

She could never have explained the chain of thought
that made her smile; but the last link in it was that her
husband in exalting his brother and depreciating himself was not altogether sincere. Kitty knew that this insin-
cerity came from his love for his brother, from his sense
of guilt at being too happy, and above all from his per-
sistent craving to be better—she loved this in him, and
so she smiled.

Her disbelief in his dissatisfaction with himself
rejoiced him. . . .[30]

Kitty's simple faith and the acting out of that faith come
together in her encounter with Levin's dying brother, Nikolai. Kitty treats Nikolai as an eternal soul, full of meaning,
just as she treats her husband. In fact, she assigns more
meaning to them both than they assume for themselves.
Kitty sees infinite value in Nikolai, although—or perhaps
especially because—he is about to depart this life, and
treats him accordingly. This is somewhat reminiscent of

Mother Teresa's attitude to the dying. She treats each one as if he or she was Jesus. As we have seen, this treatment of the sick is common to women in literature, and this is certainly a reflection of women in real life, although not every woman is equally gifted in this area—just as not all men would react as Levin does. In Kitty's case, keeping meaning for Nikolai is inspired by compassion as keeping meaning for Levin is inspired by love.

> On seeing the sick man, she was filled with pity for him. And pity in her womanly heart produced not the horror and loathing that it did in her husband but a need for action, a need to find out all the details of his condition and to remedy them. And since she had not the slightest doubt that it was her duty to help him, she had no doubt either that she could help him, and so she set to work without delay. . . . Levin found the invalid lying back on his pillows and everything around him completely changed. . . . There was a new expression of hope on his face as he gazed steadily at Kitty, not taking his eyes off her . . . Kitty evidently did not think, and had no time to think, about herself.[31]

Ultimately, the Keeper of Meaning must know that death is not the end of life and that life is good. Therefore, while facing deadly illness in oneself or a loved one may be the cause of grief, fear, and pain, it does not contain the horror that Levin experiences. As another Tolstoy character, Ivan Ilych, realizes at the moment of death: "There was no fear because there was no death. In place of death there was light."[32]

> If for this life only we have hoped in Christ, we are of all men most to be pitied. But in fact Christ has been raised from the dead.
>
> 1 Corinthians 15:19–20

62

"Thou hast hid these things from the wise and prudent, and hast revealed them unto babes." So Levin thought about his wife as he talked with her that evening. . . . He knew, too, that many great and virile minds, whose thoughts on death he had read, had brooded over it and yet did not know one hundredth part of what his wife and Agatha Mikhalovna knew.[33]

Bobbie in *The Railway Children*
Edith Nesbit

"Don't you think it's rather nice to think that we're in a book that God's writing? If I were writing a book, I might make mistakes. But God knows how to make the story end just right—in the way that's best for us."

"Do you really believe that, Mother?" Peter asked quietly.

"Yes," she said, "I do believe it—almost always—except when I'm so sad that I can't believe anything. But even when I can't believe it, I know it's true—and I try to believe it. You don't know how I try, Peter. Now take the letters to the post and don't let's be sad any more. Courage, courage! That's the finest of all the virtues!"

Edith Nesbit[34]

This life's dim windows of the soul
Distort the heavens from pole to pole
And leads you to believe a lie
When you see with, not through, the eye.

William Blake[35]

Thomas Aquinas refers to "the love of well-wishing." One who has this quality has discovered the essence of love and of trust in God—an other-consciousness that stands in radical opposition to narcissism.[36] Edith Nesbit (1858–1924) had a gift for portraying authentic and extremely appealing children. She was able to see the world through their eyes, almost as if she was one of them. The appeal of her characters is found in their combination of humor and goodness. In addition to their adventures together, these children have a lighthearted perspective. They are funny and are, with a few exceptions, so very *kind*. Bobbie of *The Railway Children* differs from the rest of our Keepers of Meaning in that she is a child of about twelve or thirteen. However, at an age when so many are self-absorbed, Bobbie has a remarkable other-consciousness combined with a generous spirit. Moreover, Bobbie encourages the reader to let *the heart see through the eye*.

As a Keeper of Meaning, she often sees things others do not and acts accordingly. These actions are sometimes misunderstood, but one of Bobbie's outstanding qualities is that she sacrifices the need to be understood. This requires a degree of inner peace that is very rare; it is something many people admire but find difficult to imitate. There are several times when Bobbie sees her own need to be understood as subordinate to other factors. This ability to "put herself in someone else's shoes," to sacrifice her natural need for understanding by those she loves best, and her "love of well-wishing" are worthy of imitation.

Bobbie, her brother, Peter, and their sister, Phyllis, go to live in the country with their mother when their father is taken to prison for a crime he did not commit. The children have not been told the reason for their father's disappearance (although Bobbie discovers it later), but they do know that their mother is worried and burdened.

Bobbie not only sees her mother's pain but does what she believes is best for her mother and from her mother's point of view, not necessarily for herself. Of course Bobbie wants to know why their lives have been turned upside down, but she also sees that her mother is doing her best to create a secure atmosphere for her children and trusts her mother to keep what secrets she must.

> But when Bobbie crept down later to bring up her presents—for she felt she really could not be separated from them all night—Mother was not writing, but leaning her head on her arms and her arms on the table. I think it was rather good of Bobbie to slip quietly away, saying over and over, "She doesn't want me to know she's unhappy, and I won't know; I won't know." But it made a sad end to the birthday.[37]

When she sees grief welling up in her mother and that her mother might not be able to hide it, Bobbie runs away, not caring whether she is misunderstood or not:

> "How tired you look, Mammy," she said; "lean on me."
> "It's my place to give Mother my arm," said Peter. "I'm the head man of the family when Father's away."
> Mother took the arm of each.
> "How awfully nice," said Phyllis, skipping joyfully, "to think of the dear Russian embracing his long-lost wife. The baby must have grown a lot since we saw her."
> "Yes," said Mother.
> "I wonder whether Father will think *I've* grown," Phyllis went on, skipping still more gaily. "I have grown already, haven't I Mother?"
> "Yes," said Mother, "oh, yes," and Bobbie and Peter felt her hands tighten on their arms.
> "Poor old Mammy, you *are* tired," said Peter.
> Bobbie said, "Come on, Phil; I'll race you to the gate."

And she started the race, though she hated doing it. *You* know why Bobbie did that. Mother only thought that Bobbie was tired of walking slowly. Even Mothers, who love you better than anyone else ever will, don't always understand.[38]

Similarly, when Phyllis mentions her grandmother at a time when her mother is very alone and must take care of the family without her husband, Bobbie sees the implications and wants to protect her mother:

"Are you fonder of us than Granny was of you when you were little?" Phyllis asked. Bobbie made signs to her to stop, but Phyllis never did see signs, no matter how plain they might be.

Mother did not answer for a minute. She got up to put more water in the teapot.

"No one," she said at last, "ever loved anyone more than my mother loved me."

Then she was quiet again, and Bobbie kicked Phyllis hard under the table, because Bobbie understood a little bit the thoughts that were making Mother so quiet—the thoughts of the time when Mother was a little girl and was all the world to *her* mother. It seems so easy and natural to run to Mother when one is in trouble. Bobbie understood a little how people do not leave off running to their mothers when they are in trouble even when they are grown up, and she thought she knew a little what it must be to be sad, and have no mother to run to any more.[39]

In her mother, Bobbie also has a model of courage, perseverance, and love. What a precious gift for all of the children to have, especially in the absence of their father. Bobbie clearly admires her mother, but that admiration is inseparable from love. "Oh, Mother," she whispered all to herself as she got into bed, "how brave you are! How I love you! Fancy being brave enough to laugh when you're feeling like *that!*[40] There are some people whom it is easy to love; the relationship is a tree already in full bloom. With others love is a choice that can bear great fruit.

Bobbie's mother models virtue, and Bobbie, living in such an atmosphere, unconsciously imitates her. The local doctor, while speaking to Peter about how to treat women, has this to say:

> "And their hearts are soft, too," the Doctor went on, "and things that we shouldn't think anything of hurt them dreadfully. So that a man has to be very careful, not only of his fists, but of his words. They're awfully brave, you know," he went on. "Think of Bobbie waiting alone in the tunnel with that poor chap. It's an odd thing—the softer and more easily hurt a woman is the better she can screw herself up to do what *has* to be done. I've seen some brave women—your Mother's one," he ended abruptly.[41]

Even Bobbie's freedom from the need to be understood is partly the result of observing that same freedom in her mother. There is a point in the story where Bobbie is, by any standard, a true heroine, having with her brother and sister saved a train full of people from crashing into a landslide. Her pride in this action is superseded by the horror of the potential catastrophe, and there is also some discomfort borne of humility at receiving so much praise. She is feeling all of this but does not give expression to her thoughts, only urging the others to leave as quickly as possible and changing the subject. (It should always be remembered that the Keeper of Meaning does little self-analysis: Bobbie is not thinking, "I'm being humble now and I hope the others are impressed by it.")

Phyllis enjoyed herself thoroughly. She had never been a real heroine before, and the feeling was delicious. Peter's ears got very red. Yet he, too, enjoyed himself. Only Bobbie wished they all wouldn't. She wanted to get away.

"You'll hear from the Company about this, I expect," said the Station Master.

Bobbie wished she might never hear of it again. She pulled at Peter's jacket.

"Oh, come away, come away! I want to go home," she said.

So they went. And as they went Station Master and Porter and guards and driver and fireman and passengers sent up a cheer.

"Oh, listen," cried Phyllis, "that's for *us!*"

"Yes," said Peter. "I say, I am glad I thought about something red and waving it."

"How lucky we *did* put on our red flannel petticoats!" said Phyllis.

Bobbie said nothing. She was thinking of the horrible mound, and the trustful train rushing towards it.

"And it was *us* that saved them," said Peter.

"How dreadful if they had all been killed!" said Phyllis, "wouldn't it, Bobbie?"

"We never got any cherries, after all," said Bobbie.

The others thought her rather heartless.[42]

Far from heartless, Bobbie is as brokenhearted over the absence of her father as the rest of the family. She is comforted by the love of her family and the faith modeled by her mother ("Dears, when you say your prayers, I think you might ask God to show His pity upon all prisoners and captives"[43]; "All we can do, you and I and Daddy, is to be brave, and patient, and"—she spoke very softly—"to pray, Bobbie, dear."[44]); by a growing hope that all will be well with her father; and by her special ability to sympathize with the brokenhearted and crushed in spirit and to take action.

Bobbie, as a Keeper of Meaning, has a vivid imagination. As we have seen in her relationship with her mother, she is able to observe behavior and see pain, suffering, or joy with the eyes of her heart that others do not even guess at. And this is certainly not limited to her mother. Her sympathy, always followed by action, is manifested time and again, as in the case of the mysterious Russian gentleman who appears at the train station, clearly in need of help and compassion:

> I do not know whether the man understood her words, but he understood the touch of the hand she thrust into his, and the kindness of the other hand that stroked his shabby sleeve. . . . Bobbie got between the others and the stranger, for she had seen that he was crying.
>
> By a most unusual piece of good fortune she had a handkerchief in her pocket. By a still more uncommon accident the handkerchief was moderately clean. Standing in front of the stranger, she got the handkerchief and passed it on to him so that the others did not see.[45]

A less dramatic but no less important instance is on the occasion of Bobbie's birthday when she thinks that Peter has given her his prized toy train engine filled with candy and then learns that he only meant to give the candy:

> Bobbie could not help her face changing a little—not so much because she was disappointed at not getting the engine, as because she had thought it so very noble of Peter, and now she felt she had been silly to think it. Also she felt she must have seemed greedy to expect the engine as well as the sweets. So her face changed. Peter saw it. He hesitated a minute; then his face changed,

too, and he said: "I mean not *all* the engine. I'll let you go halves if you like."

"You're a brick," cried Bobbie; "it's a splendid present." She said no more aloud, but to herself she said:

"That was awfully decent of Peter because I know he didn't mean to. Well, the broken half shall be my half of the engine, and I'll get it mended and give it back to Peter for his birthday."—"Yes, Mother dear, I should like to cut the cake," she added, and tea began.[46]

Bobbie *does* get help for the Russian gentleman, who is restored to his family; she *does* get Peter's engine mended; and she *does* seek help for her father from a trusted and influential friend—and is rewarded in that search. As her mother acts out of hope when her life changes so dramatically, so Bobbie acts out of hope when everything seems bleak. Thus, hope takes precedence over despair: "If it was a false hope, it was none the less a very radiant one that lay warm at Bobbie's heart, and through the days that followed lighted her little face as a Japanese lantern is lighted by a candle within."[47]

Bobbie keeps meaning for herself and those around her by seeing through her eyes into the hearts of others, sacrificing the need to be understood and acting to meet the real needs of others from their perspective, not her own. Edith Nesbit makes it quite easy for the reader to see the "love of well-wishing" that characterizes Bobbie. It is difficult to speak of something at once so simple and so deep, but the power in it is sufficient to change the world.

> She was quite oddly anxious to make other people happy. And she could keep a secret, a tolerably rare accomplishment. Also she had the power of silent sympathy. That sounds rather dull, I know, but it's not so dull as it sounds. . . . This needs practice. It is not as easy

as you might think. . . . Bobbie had another quality which you will hear differently described by different people. Some of them call it interfering in other people's business—and some call it "helping lame dogs over stiles", and some call it "loving-kindness." It just means trying to help people.[48]

While the Keeper of Meaning imitates the Savior by valuing others as He values us, she or he is not God. No person should look to a Keeper of Meaning for his or her identity; the only One who can *bestow* meaning is God Himself. Each person must look up to the Creator for the answer to the question: "Who am I?" Similarly, the Keeper of Meaning, or one who seeks to be strengthened in this area, must seek what is needed in prayer from the only One who can give such gifts. While hoping to serve others, she is not assuming responsibility for another or subjugating herself to any but the will of God. Each individual soul is the territory of God alone, and we can feel safe entrusting our souls to God's care. Indeed, it can only benefit others if we spend less energy worrying about our own well-being and focus our attention upward and outward.

The Keeper of Meaning seeks to be free from the prison of self, and there is only one key to the prison: Jesus Christ. "He who finds his life will lose it, and he who loses his life for my sake will find it" (Matt. 10:39). We can and should practice the presence of the One who gives meaning, purpose, and identity to every living thing.

In addition, and in keeping with the true self found in God, the Keeper of Meaning needs the ability to accept herself and the inner peace that comes with it, so that she does not feel the need to place a personal agenda on other people's behavior. Instead, she can see what is important to another person, knowing that soul is separate from her own. A good imagination, not so much in the creative sense as in the ability to "read between the lines" or to know that "there is more to be seen than meets the eye," is also necessary. Most of all, the desire to imitate Christ, as outlined in the introduction to this chapter, is essential.

All of these things can and should be prayed for. "If any of you lacks wisdom, let him ask God, who gives to all men generously and without reproaching, and it will be given him" (James 1:5). Both humility and a longing for great things are needed. The Keeper of Meaning must leave cynicism behind (was God cynical when He sent His Son to die for us?), but she must be realistic about how completely dependent she is on God.

An attitude of receptivity and trust is an intrinsic part of being a Keeper of Meaning and of being a woman of God. This is one of the reasons women are so particularly well adapted to perceiving and keeping meaning. Some women perceive meaning without knowing from whence that meaning comes; the Christian woman perceives meaning and knows the One who bestows it. She trusts the God who keeps her and the world in His hands, and trusts the heart He made and wherein He dwells. God refers to our "hearts" many times in the Scriptures. He knows that this is not an abstract concept but a real part of His creation. The Keeper of Meaning must entrust her heart to God's care and then have the faith to believe that He does indeed live within and is trustworthy. She also must believe that others have hearts capable of being indwelled by God. This is the glory of humanity: "the mystery hidden for ages and generations but now made manifest to his saints . . . Christ in you, the hope of glory" (Col. 1:26–27).

As we have seen from our look at Anne, Kitty, and Bobbie, the Keeper of Meaning today must be willing to learn from the past. From these characters, we learn a great deal about the infinite meaning with which God has invested the world. First, perceiving meaning is often motivated by love and compassion. Second, individual choice matters enormously. This is frequently reflected in nineteenth- and early twentieth-century literature, when the implications of one person's moral choice are placed above social trends or abstract themes. Third, faith matters. All of the novels discussed were written against the backdrop of faith in Christianity that was so much a part of the Western world at that time; certainly Austen, Tolstoy, and Nesbit had a personal faith in God that was unmistakable and appealing. These people of faith saw others as possessing an eternal soul, as did the characters they created. Fourth, it is possible to choose doing the right thing before being understood and possible to choose words carefully, sometimes being silent altogether.

The Keeper of Meaning recognizes falsehood and is concerned with protecting her own reputation or that of someone else. She sees the value of protecting virtue for both herself and others. This too may be the special province of women and one that has been woefully abandoned by many women in the present day and age. Both the ability to keep a secret and the protection of virtue are from a time gone by. On the pages of certain literary works they are preserved forever.

The characters in some novels are idealized to a certain extent; however, if we in the twenty-first century consider that to be a bad thing it is because, in the name of allegiance to "reality," we have elevated human vice to the level virtue once held. Much of today's entertainment appeals to the worst that is in humanity and normalizes the lowest common denominator so that the reader or viewer must stoop down to imitate these modern-day heroes instead of reaching up to the standard set by God. So-called "realism" is highly overrated; why must evil be considered realistic and goodness unrealistic? How often is goodness derided as shallow and boring, while in truth it is evil that may be described as repetitive and superficial? Evil is often misunderstood to be as "deep" as goodness but in a different way. No one does more to discredit this false notion than C. S. Lewis in such books as *The Screwtape Letters*, *Perelandra*, and *The Great Divorce*.

"Perfect" characters in fiction are important models for the reader. Finally, it must be kept in mind that truth is often stranger than fiction. How often have we marveled at the courage, perseverance, generosity, and other virtues found in real lives throughout history? A book written 150 years ago preserves meaning in the heart of its heroine—the meaning behind a word, a look, a secret, a death. And thank God it does.

A reason for reading these books, outside of sheer enjoyment, is to glimpse the world through the eyes of people from another time. In what ways were they different? Much emphasis in the present day is placed on career choice and fulfillment through that route, but what was the hope of fulfillment at a time when so many women did not work outside the home and extended education was available to so few? Was there rampant discontent and even despair at this lack of fulfillment, or were hope and meaning derived from an eternal source? Certainly, the meaning of life for both men and women is based on being a child of God. Perhaps the average person was less introspective years ago. Perhaps there were fewer distractions to simply *being*. Life in this world was shorter and there were fewer options. The men and women of today do indeed face an enormous challenge as they wade through the deceptions of this world, seeking peace of mind. Reading about people faced with a similar search created by people who lived in a slightly clearer atmosphere can help.

Despite the appealing aspects of a past time, the fact remains that God is the same in the twenty-first century as He was in the nineteenth century. The Holy Spirit can open the eyes of anyone's heart to see the truth about God's love for the world and how He expressed that love, as well as the potential for each life because of the cross of Christ.

If God is who Jesus proclaims Him to be, then the world is filled with meaning and hope, and the Keeper of Meaning lives day to day in such a world. Living with a conscious awareness of this truth is the great gift and responsibility of the Keeper of Meaning.

The enormous importance of human life is based on unseen realities—the existence of God and the existence of the soul. The Keeper of Meaning sees these with the eyes of his or her heart. The search for meaning will end in despair without God as the goal and center of that journey. The heart is a throne for someone; if God is not seated there, then the world, the flesh, and the devil will be worshipped. Materialism, and a reliance on the five senses to discern all of reality, is like the facade of a building with no people inside, or like a skeleton with no flesh on its bones or spirit within.

> How can I ever explain to those who insist that we must believe in the world to love it that it is *because* I disbelieve in the world that I love every breath I take, look forward with ever-greater delight to the coming of each spring, rejoice ever more in the companionship of my fellow humans. . . . To accept this world as a destination rather than a staging post, and the experience of living in it as expressing life's full significance, would seem to me to reduce life to something too banal and trivial to be taken seriously or held in esteem.[49]

For this reason I bow my knees before the Father, from whom every family in heaven and on earth is named, that according to the riches of his glory he may grant you to be strengthened with might through his Spirit in the inner man, and that Christ may dwell in your hearts through faith; that you, being rooted and grounded in love, may have power to comprehend with all the saints what is the breadth and length and height and depth, and to know the love of Christ which surpasses knowledge, that you may be filled with all the fullness of God.

Ephesians 3:14–19

Dear Father in Heaven,
I thank You for Your creation—for the beauty of Your world,
the sky, trees, rain, clouds, wind. I thank You for all of Your
reality, both seen and unseen. Thank You for all of Your chil-
dren, for human beings and the way they are made. Thank
You for my creation—for my body, my emotions, my soul,
and my thought processes. Thank You that these things are
beautiful miracles and that I can communicate with and
love other human beings, and that I can communicate with
and love You. Show me Your face in the simplest things,
especially the things I sometimes take for granted, such as
the beauties of nature.

Thank You for restoring my hope, and the hope of the
world, through the death and resurrection of Your Son.
Give me faith to believe in what I cannot see.

Please help me to embrace the truth about You and Your
creation, no matter how I am feeling. Plant the truth so
deeply in my heart that it cannot be moved, and protect
me from all deceptions of the evil one.

Open the eyes of my heart to see You at work all around me, and help me to see the infinite value of each person I encounter.

Help me to imitate Your Son, Jesus, especially in the way He treated those around Him and the way He related to You, His Father. Give me ears to hear Your voice, and give me faith to believe that You live within me. Give me the desire to listen for Your voice. Give me eyes and ears to really see and hear those around me. Help me to see beyond appearances, beyond the surface.

I pray for the gift of compassion to see the needs of others and the wisdom and strength to act on what I see. Help me, like Jesus, to have an attitude of service towards and not of power over another. Help me to be comfortable with silence and to choose words carefully.

Give me eyes to see the meaning in world events and to see You shining in the terrible darkness of this age.

Give me the freedom to be misunderstood, to not have to say everything I think, and to not think about myself all the time. I thank You that You have freed me from the prison of self.

I entrust You with the care of my soul and ask that You would bring healing where needed. Give me faith to believe in You, so that I can be free to love others as You have loved me.

In Jesus' name,
Amen.

3

The Woman of Courage

Every virtue must always be tied with all others at their core; thus there can be no bravery without truthfulness, without justice, or without discipline.

Josef Pieper[1]

God gives each of us a unique story to live out. We may be given the opportunity to risk our lives or even die for the truth, or we may be asked to face difficult daily circumstances with hope and perspective. No matter what our story is, we have the chance to grow in the virtue of courage.

The seven classic virtues—faith, hope, love, prudence, temperance, courage, and justice—are inseparable from one another. Jane Eyre could not love rightly, putting God first, without the courage to leave Mr. Rochester. Anne Elliot in her prudence, in her quiet listening and embracing of reality, allows hope to be reborn; by the same route Bobbie ennobles those around her. Kitty's faith makes her prudent (able to perceive reality); Natasha's love awakens her to a consciousness of sin and of justice. Lucy's love relationship with Aslan produces courage. And on and on. As in the case of Lucy, the Scriptures seem to say that our courage is contingent on trust in God, the same trust that produces hope: "Be strong and of good courage, do not fear or be in dread of them: for it is the LORD your God who goes with you; He will not fail you or forsake you" (Deut. 31:6). Ultimately, the perfect love of God casts out the greatest fear of all—that of being left alone in the universe, in a place where no one will ever come to fill the emptiness. It is in relationship with the God of love that that fear is dispelled forever. Thus Jesus tells us truly not to fear when we are with Him. It is in this sense that perfect love casts out fear.

It is possible to grow in virtue by practicing the spiritual disciplines—solitude, silence, fasting, frugality, chastity, secrecy, sacrifice, study, worship, celebration, service, prayer, fellowship, confession, and submission. Thus, in her silent and secret acts of service, Bobbie grows in courage regarding her difficult circumstances. In sacrificing her need for Mr. Rochester, Jane's faith actually deepens as does her capacity for love. In choosing solitude over her former way of life and an attitude of sacrifice, Natasha grows in prudence and justice. With examples like these in literature, further examples found in family, friends, and history—and most especially with the example of Jesus Himself and empowerment of the Holy Spirit—there is every reason to believe that we can grow in the virtues in the same way.

Focusing now on the virtue at hand, if we want to become more courageous, it would be helpful to understand what courage is and what it is not. Josef Pieper goes to the heart of the matter when he describes true courage in this way:

That person is brave who does not allow himself to be brought by the fear of secondary and transient evils to

the point of forsaking the final and authentic good things.
. . . Fortitude presumes to a certain extent that a man is
afraid of evil; its essence does not consist in knowing no
fear but rather in not allowing himself to be compelled
by fear into evil or to fail to accomplish the good. [2]

Thus, the person who seeks courage needs a good measure of prudence, a clear grasp of reality and the meaning at the heart of that reality. It is doing good while fully
aware of the evil in the world and what is at stake in the
life that he loves so well and in the heavenly realms.

It is possible to be genuinely brave only when all those
real or apparent assurances fail, that is, when the natural man is afraid; not, however, when he is afraid out of
unreasoning timidity, but when, with a clear view of the
real situation facing him, he cannot help being afraid,
and, indeed, with good reason. If in this supreme test,
in face of which, the braggart falls silent and every heroic
gesture is paralyzed, a man walks straight up to the cause
of his fear and is not deterred from doing that which is
good; if, moreover, he does so for the sake of the good—
which ultimately means for the sake of God, and therefore not from ambition or from fear or being taken for
a coward—this man, and he alone, is truly brave. [3]

Thus, the woman of courage does not pretend that
evil is good or ever can become good. She is able to speak
the truth when confronted by evil; chooses reality over
delusion even if she is afraid (and with reality chooses
God); knows that there are some things worse than
death and is ready to die for her faith; and lives according to an inner strength and code despite difficult circumstances or what might appear to be weakness to
others. Courage not only requires this grasp of reality
and devotion to the good but other qualities not nor-
mally associated with courage, such as patience, vul-

nerability, and cheerfulness. These will be explored more fully in this chapter.

As can be seen from these aspects of courage, anyone can become brave by imitating Jesus. Like all the other virtues, courage is not the province of men or of women but of all made in the image of God. Both men and women must follow the same One to grow in courage or any of the virtues. However, the implications for embracing courage in a truly feminine way are interesting. Women should not abdicate true courage to men because they think it is their role. Both the need to protect and the need to be protected are strong in women. However, the need for protection when one's true safety is not found first in God can degenerate into self-pity. Moreover, because women are strongly intuitive and "in touch with" their feeling being, they can learn from men by seeking to become freer to place the work God has given them to do before their feelings about it. This requires courage.

A shining example may be found in The Lord of the Rings trilogy by J. R. R. Tolkien. In that saga, the nine members of the fellowship have a quest placed before them, and all of their energies are given to fulfilling that quest. While they certainly have feelings about it, their actions are not guided by those feelings but by the task at hand. One exchange between Gandalf the Wizard and Frodo the Hobbit summarizes this perspective well:

> "I wish it need not have happened in my time," said Frodo.
>
> "So do I," said Gandalf, "and so do all who live to see such times. But that is not for them to decide. All we have to decide is what to do with the time that is given us. . . . The Enemy still lacks one thing to give him strength and knowledge to beat down all resistance,

break the last defences, and cover all the lands in a second darkness. He lacks the One Ring." . . .

"I do really wish to destroy it!" cried Frodo. "Or, well, to have it destroyed. I am not made for perilous quests. I wish I had never seen the Ring! Why did it come to me? Why was I chosen?"

"Such questions cannot be answered," said Gandalf. "You may be sure that it was not for any merit that others do not possess: not for power or wisdom, at any rate. But you have been chosen and you must therefore use such strength and heart and wits as you have."[4]

In our modern world Christians often give far too much attention to how they are feeling about God at a particular moment, and they hope that God will make them feel good, free, or at peace. God may certainly be relied upon to provide all these things, but only when we seek and serve the Giver before the Gift. It is often possible to put the healing of our own souls before God Himself. Women, who ideally are acutely aware of how soul, spirit, body, and mind work together, must be especially careful of this.

Just as women can learn from men in the growth of virtue, so can men learn from women. History and literature are full of examples of courageous women, exhibiting this virtue in uniquely feminine ways that range from the most humble setting to an all-out war between good and evil. From Joan of Arc to Corrie ten Boom, history is replete with women who were truly courageous. How true it is that one person can impact the world for good! A few examples from literature are now before us.

Elizabeth in *Pride and Prejudice*
Jane Austen

Joy's a subtle elf. I think man's happiest when he forgets himself.

Cyril Tournier[5]

Courage sometimes appears in disguises that are quite convincing. In Lizzy, courage is disguised as light-heartedness, perspective, and a sense of humor. The woman of courage does not fear death but at the same time does not despise life. Objectivity is required and a sense that there is perhaps something more important than one's own life. There is a determination to believe in a world that is bigger than one's own subjective feelings. Such a combination often produces an interesting mix of vulnerability and standards that are not open to compromise. Lizzy is also a woman who, despite her stubbornness, sees her need to change.

Elizabeth Bennet is faced with some extremely difficult circumstances, beginning with the poor model of womanhood, or even personhood, provided by her mother; the lack of guidance and strength found in her father; and the fact that she is an unmarried woman with no money in nineteenth-century England. She must be patient and trust men to take the initiative where she cannot. In the course of the story Lizzy is also faced with her sister Lydia's openly living with a man before marriage—behavior that at that period in history would ruin not only Lydia's reputation but reflect severely on that of her sisters as well, perhaps destroying their prospects of marrying into a respectable family (prospects already limited by the relative poverty of her family).

Jane Austen makes a point of describing Lizzy as one who is, by *nature,* capable of much happiness and enjoyment in life. When she overhears Darcy (the man she is destined to marry but whose apparent pride and conceit repel her through half the novel) insult her physical appearance ("She is tolerable; but not handsome enough to tempt *me*"), she "remained with no very cordial feelings towards him. She told the story with great spirit among her friends; for she had a lively, playful disposition, which delighted in anything ridiculous."[6] At another dance she learns that Wickham, the one man she hoped to see, is not coming—and this on account of Darcy—and she is disappointed. "But Elizabeth was not formed for ill-humour; and though every prospect of her own was destroyed for the evening, it could not dwell long on her spirits; and having told all her griefs to Charlotte Lucas, whom she had not seen for a week, she was soon able to make a voluntary transition to the oddities of her cousin, and to point him out to her particular notice."[7] When this same cousin, Mr. Collins, proposes to her, Elizabeth is "so near laughing that she could not use the short pause he allowed in any attempt to stop him."[8]

With a temperament such as this Lizzy is ahead of the game. However, it should by no means be assumed that her ability to respond to disappointment and trouble with humor and perspective is effortless. No good behavior in sinful humanity is without effort. There is always a choice. Nor should we excuse ourselves from imitating these characteristics if we are by nature more prone to depression, anxiety, or hypersensitivity. There is a great effort involved, and sometimes this effort will seem beyond our capacities. Indeed, it *is* beyond *our* capacities. But it is not beyond the power of God.

It is not that Lizzy is without emotion, nor does she trivialize or diminish her emotions or those of others. On the contrary, she is a woman of deep feeling and strong convictions. Everything she does is expressed with great intensity and self-assurance. She is fiercely protective of her sister Jane, whom she loves and respects, and with whom she has a wonderful friendship. She is capable of righteous anger towards Wickham, who seeks to ruin Lydia's reputation; towards Darcy, who almost ruins her sister's happiness; and towards Darcy's aunt, who tries to stand in the way of Lizzy's happiness. When Lydia runs off with Wickham, Lizzy is horrified and sickened and immediately sees how devastating this behavior is for the whole family.

Despite Lizzy's wonderful capacity to feel deeply, she is free from the tyranny of her own emotions. She is honest, outspoken, and uncompromising and seems very much at home with herself. Lizzy does not care what people whom she does not like think of her and readily speaks her mind. She even turns down Darcy's proposal of marriage because she believes him to have a character she cannot respect and because of the pain he causes her sister—a courageous act in itself, considering her lack of money and marriage prospects. Later, when the truth about Darcy's really good character begins to dawn on her, she is able to care for others despite her disappointment, to make her sister Jane laugh, and to go about her daily routine with composure. This, even while wondering if Darcy will ever love her again and yet having to patiently wait for the fulfillment or disappointment of her hopes. And when Jane's hopes for marriage with the man she loves are realized, Lizzy can rejoice with her sister even while laughing at herself.

"I am certainly the most fortunate creature that ever existed!" cried Jane. "Oh! Lizzy, why am I thus singled from my family, and blessed above them all! If I could but see *you* as happy! If there *were* but such another man for you!"

"If you were to give me forty such men, I never could be so happy as you. Till I have your disposition, your goodness, I never can have your happiness. No, no, let me shift for myself; and perhaps, if I have very good luck, I may meet with another Mr. Collins in time."[9]

While not self-absorbed, Lizzy is very pleased with her own views. Speaking to her sister Jane:

You wish to think all the world respectable, and are hurt if *I* speak ill of anybody. *I* only want to think *you* perfect, and you set yourself against it. Do not be afraid of my running into excess, of my encroaching on your privilege of universal good will. You need not. There are few people whom I really love, and still fewer of whom I think well. The more I see of the world, the more I am dissatisfied with it; and every day confirms my belief of the inconsistency of all human characters, and of the little dependence that can be placed on the appearance of either merit or sense.[10]

Indeed, she is a little too pleased with herself. Her own happiness is almost destroyed by her tendency to judge and criticize, her "prejudice." Lizzy may claim as her motto the words of Shakespeare: "This above all, to thine own self be true." However, Lizzy and Jane both are capable of self-examination and admitting to wrong. Indeed, Lizzy does so with her usual enthusiasm and even wit:

> "How despicably have I acted!" she cried. "I, who have prided myself on my discernment!—I, who have valued myself on my abilities! who have often disdained the generous candour of my sister, and gratified my vanity in useless or blameable distrust.—How humiliating is this discovery!—Yet, how just a humiliation!—Had I been in love, I could not have been more wretchedly blind. But vanity, not love, has been my folly. . . . Till this moment I never knew myself."[11]

The importance of the ability to recognize one's own sin in the pursuit of virtue cannot be overestimated. Psalm 36 states that for the wicked man "there is no fear of God before his eyes. For he flatters himself in his own eyes that his iniquity cannot be found out and hated. The words of his mouth are mischief and deceit; he has ceased to act wisely and do good. . . . He sets himself in a way that is not good; he spurns not evil" (1–3, 4).

Lizzy finds her most vulnerable place, and the place most in need of transformation, in relationship with a man. As wonderful and right as Lizzy's marriage to Darcy is, her identity apart from Darcy is well formed; in fact, this increases her appeal as a woman tremendously. She brings him great gifts in her lightheartedness and spontaneity, while he brings the integrity and depth of character missing in most of her own family.

Lizzy has the courage to realize that when all is said and done she perhaps does not know everything. She is also not the center of her own life. The willingness to bring perspective and humor to life's troubles communicates a delightful objectivity and freedom from self that requires courage and practice and is worthy of imitation.

Betsey in *David Copperfield*
Charles Dickens

> Woe to those who call evil good and good evil,
> who put darkness for light
>   and light for darkness,
> who put bitter for sweet
>   and sweet for bitter!
> Woe to those who are wise in their own eyes
>   and shrewd in their own sight!
>
> Isaiah 5:20–21

Courage does indeed come in many disguises. And no one is a master of disguise like Charles Dickens (1812–1870). He can clothe the deepest goodness, the most generous spirit, or the bravest heart—all without a hint of cynicism or irony—in the most eccentric garb imaginable. One is often completely distracted by the eccentricity of some of his most noble characters, and their outbursts of virtue initially come as a bit of a shock. After a glimpse of this virtue one is on the lookout for it, just as one gets a glimpse of the evil in other Dickens characters that is eventually fully exposed. Some of the most wonderful moments in

91

Dickens's works come when this splendid goodness comes face-to-face with this terrible evil and emerges victorious. This confrontation, and the total vanquishing of evil, make for some of the most delightful reading in all literature.

Two of these scenes may be found in *David Copperfield:* One is the scene towards the end where Micawber exposes Uriah Heep; the other is near the beginning when Betsey Trotwood exposes Mr. Murdstone. In both cases bondage to evil is broken by the speaking of truth. In the latter case the person freed from this bondage is a child. This is particularly powerful because a child is not on an equal footing with any adult and requires the protection and help of a good adult to sever the bond with evil. The good adult in this case is David's aunt, Betsey Trotwood.

What is Betsey Trotwood faced with when she meets David's stepfather? Mr. Murdstone has been described as evil. That is a strong word, and one that should not be used lightly. However, there is clear evidence from the text of *David Copperfield* to justify the use of it in his case. When Betsey is speaking of David's mother's second marriage she says, "She goes and marries a Murderer—or a man with a name like it!" Betsey is not too far from the truth. Mr. Murdstone is acutely aware of the human frailty of his wife, Clara, and her son, David. In fact, he derives energy and pleasure from using these weaknesses to inflict pain on those he professes to love. Despite this, he does not appear to be conscious of his own sin and never admits to wrongdoing of any kind. Instead, he transfers his own shame onto Clara and David, using them as scapegoats. Consequently, they both experience terrible guilt; they are so enmeshed in the evil influence of this man that they unconsciously assume his guilt, blaming themselves for some mysterious and elusive fault.

When Murdstone beats David because he has trouble with his lessons, David tries to stop him by biting him.

> He beat me then as if he would have beaten me to death. . . . How well I recollect, when I became quiet, what an unnatural stillness seemed to reign through the whole house! How well I remember, when my smart and passion began to cool, how wicked I began to feel!
>
> My stripes were sore and stiff, and made me cry afresh, when I moved; but they were nothing to the guilt I felt. It lay heavier on my breast than if I had been a most atrocious criminal I dare say. . . .
>
> I began to wonder fearfully what would be done to me. Whether it was a criminal act that I had committed? Whether I should be taken into custody, and sent to prison?[12]

The guilt over this episode is so tremendous that he is in torment until he can beg his mother to forgive him. When he finally has an opportunity to do this, Clara is so much under the control of Murdstone that she believes in David's guilt as heartily as David does: "Oh Davy," she said. "That you could hurt any one I love! Try to be better, pray to be better! I forgive you; but I am so grieved, Davy, that you should have such bad passions in your heart."[13] Murdstone has chosen Clara as his special object of control, and Clara is willing to do almost anything to keep him happy. Since he despises any show of emotion or gentleness, her true nature is quickly crushed as he succeeds in blackmailing her with his own rage and hate. He particularly hates any sign of tenderness or understanding towards David, and he uses mother and son against each other.

Two people glimpse Murdstone's real nature—David and the servant Peggotty. Clara either cannot or will not see Peggotty's rather blatant hints about this man's true character, but Murdstone hates and must eliminate anyone who sees the truth. Eventually Peggotty must go, and David, who with the keen observation of a child, makes it impossible for Murdstone to hide from his own sin, is subject to physical abuse and emotional torture and is finally sent away to endure further miseries. Murdstone has succeeded in surrounding himself with women (Clara and his own sister who lives with them) who will not smash the illusion of his own perfection. This inability to acknowledge his own sin is what makes Murdstone an evil man. Not only this, but he systematically destroys those he professes to love. The only people he can tolerate are those who perpetuate his lie.

The key to drawing near to God, and to others, is the ability to say "I am sorry." These three words are, in many ways, more important than "I love you."

> The evil deny the suffering of their guilt—the painful awareness of their sin, inadequacy, and imperfection— by casting their pain onto others through projection and scapegoating. They themselves may not suffer, but those around them do. They cause suffering. The evil create for those under their dominion a miniature sick society. . . . It is consistently true that the evil do not *appear* to suffer deeply. Because they cannot admit to weakness or imperfection in themselves, they must appear that way. They must appear to themselves to be continually on top of things, continually in command. Their narcissism demands it.[14]

The most important person in David's life, both before and after Murdstone's arrival, is his mother. She is a very affectionate and loving person, and much is made of her gentle, pliant nature and her youth and inexperience. "Mr. Copperfield had . . . told her, when she doubted herself, that a loving heart was better and stronger than wisdom, and that he was a happy man in hers."[15] The fact remains, however, that she watches her son being abused by a sadistic, evil man and does nothing. "I thought that my mother was sorry to see me standing in the room so scared and strange, and that, presently, when I stole to a chair, she followed me with her eyes more sorrowfully still—missing, perhaps, some freedom in my childish tread—but the word was not spoken, and the time for it was gone."[16]

As is true of so many other aspects of *David Copperfield,* the creation of Clara may be a reflection of Dickens's ambivalent feelings towards his own mother—at once loving and innocent, and capable of betrayal and abandonment. "His relationship to his mother was central to his life, but it was necessarily a complex one established upon guilt and rejection but combined with a kind of hopeless love."[17] Although her own spirit is killed in the process ("I think she got to be more timid, and more frightened-like, of late; and that a hard word was like a blow to her"),[18] Clara supports her husband in his decisions. It would not be too much to say that Murdstone hates David to the point of wanting to kill him by putting him in situations that might ultimately cause his death. But Clara is either too enthralled with her husband or too frightened of him to protect her son. This does not appear to be a case of a young woman wanting to leave an abusive husband in the nineteenth century and having no escape route.

Clara's need for Murdstone's love and approval is so enormous that she essentially abandons her child. It is tragic that Clara is in bondage to this evil, and all the more so because she cannot protect David, who is completely reliant on the adults around him. When submission to evil reaches this level, and the false feminine in Clara meets the false masculine in Murdstone, destruction is the result. To separate from evil can literally be a matter of life and death. In this case, enmeshment rather than separation results in disaster.

Clara displays a remarkable lack of wisdom and discernment; she has never assumed her full identity as a woman and attempts to gain her identity from her husband, putting her true self to death. Murdstone conceals his true nature before the marriage (although David and Peggotty sense that something is wrong the moment they meet him). Like all human beings, Clara needs kindness and affection and continues to believe she will receive this from her new husband, despite daily evidence to the contrary. Clara does not live long after the birth of Murdstone's child, and were it not for Betsey Trotwood, it is difficult to say what would have become of David.

After his mother's death, David's journey takes him to school and then to work with other boys in the London warehouse of Murdstone's wine trade. Finding this life unendurable David "forms a resolution"—to run away and seek his Aunt Betsey (a remarkably brave thing to do considering he has never met her, he is virtually penniless, and she lives sixty miles away). The little money that he had and all his belongings are stolen at the outset, and he walks to Dover from London, arriving on his aunt's doorstep starving and in rags. There is not room here to give a complete description of Betsey Trotwood and her eccentric and highly entertaining behavior. However, it must be said that she treats David with the utmost kindness. This, and her wonderful discernment about people are some of the hallmarks of her character. From the moment of David's meeting with his aunt, his future begins to brighten; in Betsey Trotwood, Edward Murdstone has met his match.

Betsey is extremely outspoken and honest; indeed, one gets the impression that she says anything that comes into her head. Fortunately, she also has the abil-

ity to see people for who they really are. In George Mac-
Donald's story *The Princess and Curdie,* Curdie is able
to feel the true nature of people by touching their hands.
While shaking hands with a person he may feel the
scales of a snake or the talons of a vulture. In Betsey's
case it is as if her eyes are opened to see into people's
hearts. Murdstone tells Betsey that David is sullen, rebel-
lious, violent, and intractable. Betsey does not believe a
word of it; she knows David too well already. Her friend,
Mr. Dick, is considered by many to be mad; she knows
he is not and indeed seeks his advice above all others.
David has not related his treatment at the hands of Mr.
Murdstone to his aunt; he merely says that Murdstone
has never liked him or been kind to him. As Murdstone
gives his version of the story, Betsey eyes him keenly,
observes him narrowly, and "listened with the closest
attention, sitting perfectly upright, with her hands
folded on one knee, and looking grimly on the speaker."[19]
Betsy replies to Murdstone with these words, the power
of which can hardly be overestimated.

"Do you think I don't know," said my aunt, turning a
deaf ear to the sister, and continuing to address the
brother, and to shake her head at him with infinite
expression, "what kind of life you must have led that
poor, unhappy, misdirected baby? . . . Do you think I
can't understand you as well as if I had seen you," pursued my aunt, "now that I *do* see you and hear you—
which I tell you candidly, is anything but a pleasure to
me? . . . He was made of sweetness. He worshipped her.
He doted on her boy—tenderly doted on him! He was to
be another father to him, and they were all to live
together in a garden of roses, weren't they? Ugh! Get
along with you, do! . . .
"And when you had made sure of the poor little fool,"
said my aunt—"God forgive me that I should call her so,
and she gone where *you* won't go in a hurry—because

you had not done wrong enough to her and hers, you begin to train her, must you? begin to break her, like a poor caged bird, and wear her deluded life away, in teaching her to sing *your* notes?

"Mr. Murdstone," she said, shaking her finger at him, "you were a tyrant to the simple baby, and you broke her heart. She was a loving baby—I know that; I knew it years before *you* ever saw her—and through the best part of her weakness you gave her the wounds she died of. There is the truth for your comfort, however you like it. . . .

"That was the time, Mr. Murdstone, when she gave birth to her boy here," said my aunt; "to the poor child you sometimes tormented her through afterwards, which is a disagreeable remembrance, and makes the sight of him odious now. Aye! aye! You needn't wince!" said my aunt. "I know it's true without that."

He had stood by the door, all this while, observant of her, with a smile upon his face, though his black eyebrows were heavily contracted. I remarked now, that, though the smile was on his face still, his colour had gone in a moment, and he seemed to breathe as if he had been running.[20]

With this speech, Betsey Trotwood is speaking the truth and thus exposing the lie. And there is no doubt that on some level Murdstone knows it, for he winces when he realizes that he has been found out. Surely if he ever hated David and Peggotty for making him catch a glimpse of his sin, he hates Betsey even more for giving a name to it. She calls him a tyrant who deliberately took advantage of Clara's weakness, crushed her spirit, and was a direct cause of her death. She says the reason he cannot bear to look at David is that doing so reminds him of his sin against his wife—a sin he cannot face and still maintain his self-image of perfection. She also knows that while Clara was a loving person with a kind and generous heart, she was also deluded and made a grave mistake in marrying Murdstone. She then dismisses Murdstone, takes David into her care, and provides an atmosphere of truth and hope. When he leaves to go to school, her words to him are these: "Never . . . be mean in anything; never be false; never be cruel."[21] The bondage to evil has been broken in two ways—separation from the evil person, and the speaking of the truth.

Evil can be confusing, intimidating, and even compelling for some who are not free in Christ or who have a close connection with someone evil in their past or present. In Mr. Murdstone we see evidence of evil behavior. It is vital to recognize evil in order to remain separate from it, to help others as Betsey does, and to see places where one might have been touched by evil in the past. We must not excuse evil or think it can become good. Nor must we give too much attention to evil. If we focus on God, the author of goodness, evil will be exposed and routed. "Resist the devil and he will flee from you. Draw near to God and He will draw near to you" (James 4:7–8). Recognizing goodness and surrounding ourselves with it is key to the Christian faith and to recognizing the face of God if one is seeking Him.

> Finally, brethren, whatever is true, whatever is honorable, whatever is just, whatever is pure, whatever is lovely, whatever is gracious, if there is any excellence, if there is anything worthy of praise, think about these things.
>
> Philippians 4:8

One of the results of reading good fiction where the objective nature of good and evil is recognized is that there will be less confusion and deception when these are encountered in life. It is equally vital for Christians

to know the treasures that are theirs because they belong
to Jesus: a new identity in Christ; the indwelling Holy
Spirit who brings sanctification; the Word of God in the
Bible—the truth that replaces the lies in our lives; the
community of believers; the power of prayer.

Why is it courageous to do as Betsey Trotwood did?
She acts out of her true identity and does not seek to
find it in another creature; the need for approval, an
unruffled existence, and fear of conflict do not super-
sede speaking the truth. We have all been in places where
we should have spoken up but did not. Betsey fully recognizes the evil before her, but she acts anyway on behalf
of a child. This is an act of service to others; such service is a key part of true courage.

Pauline in *Descent into Hell*
Charles Williams

Choosing Reality Instead of Illusion

The coward who tries to be brave is before the man who is brave because he is made so, and never had to try.

George MacDonald[22]

Pauline Anstruther, the heroine of the 1937 novel *Descent into Hell* by Charles Williams (1886–1945), is offered a choice between living in relationship and living in solitude. It is not easy to choose rightly; she is afraid of her true self, ennobled by God, and of His awesome power. "And if things are terrifying . . . can they be good?"[23] she asks. Yet from the beginning of the novel, Pauline is being drawn by God towards abundant life. Although Williams speaks in this book of "the Omnipotence" and not of Christ, Pauline is called to choose what bears a strong resemblance to the Christian life, characterized not only by committed relationships with God and others but by forgiveness, love, dependence, and sacrifice. While the setting is fairly commonplace—a group of people in a suburb of London who have gathered to produce a play—Pauline's choice is couched in such supernatural terms as only Charles Williams can integrate into a contemporary setting with authenticity.

Indeed, this is one of his unique gifts as a writer, one he uses to great effect and sometimes to great peril, as we shall see. *Descent into Hell* is a complex book that communicates several powerful themes. There are many characters in the book, but we shall concentrate on Pauline and the two people who are calling her in opposite directions: Paul Stanhope, who calls her to engagement with others and with God, and Lily Sammile, who calls her to the false hope of happiness in an illusory world in which Pauline is the only inhabitant—a descent into the hell of self-love and unreality. Another character, Wentworth, does go down this latter path, divorcing himself from God, other human beings, and soon all of reality; living in a fantasy world eventually fails to satisfy him, and his soul is lost. His story stands in sharp contrast to Pauline's.

The choice before Wentworth and Pauline stands before us all: engaging with others and God or finding comfort in a fantasy world where everything and everyone is motivated by our own need. Without the freedom from the self, found in Christ, each of us could potentially become a Wentworth. However, it is important to note that fantasy and illusion are different from imagination, which is a wonderful gift from God. In the world of fantasy our purpose is to gratify our desires, and this in isolation. We are the center of everything and everyone in our created world. Illusion is stale, repetitive, and ultimately empty. The true imagination, on the other hand, is creative and fruitful and often leads to hope. It is focused on good and beautiful things outside of the self and is concerned with objective reality.

Williams introduces the supernatural element through Pauline in the early pages of the novel; for years she has been confronted with another Pauline, an exact twin whom she sees approaching and from whom she runs in terror. "I have a trick," she says, "of meeting an exact likeness of myself in the street."[24] She lives in fear of meeting herself because, although she is not entirely unconscious of it, she has succeeded in diminishing or dampening certain aspects of herself—the capacity to be known by God and to know Him, and the freedom to experience real joy and sacrificial love.

Pauline's true self, who relentlessly pursues her, demands a level of engagement with the world and a loss of control that have been unacceptable to Pauline. She is terrified both of what God can give her and what He may require of her. It is easier to recognize no duty to anyone, no service to others, and no dependence based on her own need. "Why do you refuse to lean?"[25] her grandmother asks her. There is a tendency within Pauline to guard her heart as if it is a pitcher filled with water; if she gives this water away it will never be replenished and she will be left dry. There is also a tendency to dampen the flame of her spirit in a manner similar to continually snuffing a candle flame because of fear of fire. However, she is seeking and longing and seems to suspect that the time is fast approaching when she must face herself. First, she has to realize that something good can also be frightening. Suffering is not necessarily the bad thing to be avoided at all costs, as Mrs. Sammile would have her believe. Stanhope helps her to see that the inevitable encounter with herself may prove to be a blessing, despite the fact that it is fearful.

I can witness to the truth of this from my own life, when at the age of twenty-seven I finally had to face some painful experiences and emotions from my past. Burying these for so many years had taken a heavy toll on my mind, heart, and soul, but it was the love of God that called me to find Him in the reality of all that I had suffered and slowly to find anything illusory not only not appealing but actually repelling and even frightening. There were many times when I found it hard to believe that the terror I experienced when I crashed into reality could be a good thing. But I learned that it was a better thing than sitting on top of this terror, year after year, as if it did not exist. And the answer to all of this lay in the cross, where I could bring all of my sin and suffering and receive the life of Jesus in return. I also began to see Jesus bring my true self to life again, at times a frightening experience that would cause me to seek refuge in old patterns of behavior that felt "safe," as Pauline is compelled to do. However, like Pauline, I found it increasingly difficult to stay there for long without knowing that something was "off," without a lack of authenticity. I had come too far into the light to pretend to be the "old man" and make it convincing, even to myself.

Stanhope calls Pauline to God and to a new level of love between human beings, a level that involves willingness to both give and receive help. Her salvation ultimately comes to depend on her willingness to allow her burden of fear to be carried by another, and by her willingness to carry another's fear. Williams does truly understand the *nature* of salvation and the *sort* of thing it is. In fact, he may convey this better than any other writer of fiction and certainly in a most unique fashion. He also has a profound understanding of human nature as created by God and what sort of behavior and belief will produce either happiness or misery. He understands the importance of the physical creation and of the body that can lead us to glory or degradation. However, he does not understand, or at least does not convey here, the *fact* of salvation as offered by God to the world in Christ. Not that he pretends to; Stanhope plainly tells Pauline that there is "no need to introduce Christ, unless you wish."[26] But since Williams deals so directly with

Christian themes, it is important to make distinctions as to what is Christian and what is not.

When Pauline tells Stanhope of her fear of meeting herself, he assures her that she has no reason to fear; he will be afraid for her. "Listen—when you go from here, when you're alone, when you think you'll be afraid, let me put myself in your place, and be afraid instead of you."[27] How often some of us would like to have done just this for a loved one! I have known mothers who long to do this for their children. God Himself wants to carry the burdens of His children.

We are indeed to bear one another's burdens and to suffer and rejoice with one another. We are to imitate Jesus in His attitude of service and sacrifice and imitate Him in our love for others. As we walk with someone who is suffering, we point them to Jesus, who died to heal their pain and save their soul. Each person's journey is his or her own, and the effects of suffering on someone else's behalf can be devastating. The effects on the person in pain are tragic as well, for they would miss their appointed meeting with Christ in that dark time and fail to see the wonder of His healing power as they take their stand with Him on the cross and in the resurrection that follows.

Paul Stanhope is literally feeling Pauline's fear instead of her. This is contrary to Christian doctrine that says only God Himself, through Jesus' death on the cross, and out of love for us, can bear our sufferings and give His peace in return. In *Descent into Hell* Williams describes Stanhope's experience of taking Pauline's fear, and Pauline is indeed relieved of it. The substitution works. "It was necessary first intensely to receive all her spirit's conflict. . . . The body of his flesh received her alien terror, his mind carried the burden of her world."[28] Further, Pauline finds her salvation by the same means when she in turn takes on the fear of an ancestor, John

Struther, who was martyred and burned at the stake centuries before. Pauline Anstruther and John Struther
have an encounter, and both find their salvation in this
act of sacrificial love.

> "Lord God, I cannot bear the fear of the fire."
> She said: "What fire?" and still with his back to her
> he answered: "The fire they will burn me in to-day unless
> I say what they choose. Lord God, take away the fear if
> it be thy will. Lord God, be merciful to a sinner. Lord
> God, make me believe."
> She was here. She had been taught what to do. She
> had her offer to make now and it would not be refused.
> She herself was offered, in a most certain fact, through
> four centuries, her place at the table of exchange. . . .
> Behind her, her own voice said: "Give it to me, John
> Struther." . . . He fell on his knees, and in a great roar of
> triumph he called out: "I have seen the salvation of my
> God."[29]

It is important to not misunderstand how God gives
to us and how we give to others. Pauline's act is not John
Struther's salvation. One is reminded in this story of the
martyrdom of Joan of Arc, who, when she was dying at
the stake, called out to friends standing by to place a
crucifix at eye level that she might gaze upon it. If
Pauline had lived in John Struther's time, she might have
done the same for him. But she cannot suffer for him.
It is equally important to note that Charles Williams
does *not* believe we can bear the *sins* of others. "He
endured her sensitiveness, but not her sin; the substitution there, if indeed there is a substitution, is hidden
in the central mystery of Chirstendom which Christen-
dom itself has never understood, nor can."[30]
From this it should not be supposed that we are not
to imitate Christ in His example of sacrificial love. We
are called to stand with one another in sorrow and joy,

rejoicing with those who rejoice and grieving with those who grieve. However, there is no human being who can suffer for us. Williams is confusing sacrificial love with substitution and a very necessary dependence on others with salvation through them. We have to go through difficult things, not around them, and Christ walks with us and remains with us when we emerge on the other side.

The lasting truth of what has happened for Pauline in this encounter lies in this—that, believing in God, she was willing to stand with someone in their time of suffering despite her own fear, and that she was willing to acknowledge her own need and accept the help of a fellow human being in her own suffering. Both of these require courage. This is indeed grace from God, acted out in human relationship.

> Ashamed of betrayal, unashamed of repentance and dependence, she sprang . . . For the first time in her young distracted life her energy leapt to a natural freedom of love.[31]

> She who had made a duty of her arrogance had found a duty in her need. . . . At precisely the moment when she could have done without him she went to ask for him.[32]

In choosing this path, despite her fear, she has embraced reality in a new way and is ready to meet her true self and be integrated with her, a glorious experience.

> She opened her eyes again; there—as a thousand times in her looking-glass—there! The ruffled brown hair, the long nose, the firm compressed mouth, the tall body, the long arms, her dress, her gesture. It wore no supernatural splendour of aureole, but its rich nature burned and glowed before her, bright as if mortal flesh had indeed

become what all lovers know it to be. Its colour bewildered by its beauty; its voice was Pauline's, as she had wished it to be for pronouncing the imagination of the grand art. But no verse, not Stanhope's, not Shakespeare's, not Dante's, could rival the original, and this was the original, and the verse was but the best translation of a certain manner of its life. The glory of poetry could not outshine the clear glory of the certain fact, and not any poetry could hold as many meanings as the fact. One element coordinated original and translation; that element was joy . . . her incapacity for joy had admitted fear, and fear had imposed separation.[33]

She now has a greater capacity for joy, as well as sorrow, and is ready to deal better with human frailty in herself and others. She is shunning illusion and embracing solid, flesh and blood reality with all of its capacity to disappoint and inspire, to hurt and to love. Most of all, Pauline is no longer afraid of reality, even if it is difficult. She has no longing for what is *not* and even finds the idea absurd.

It is this realm of *what is not* that is Mrs. Sammile's territory. There is a restlessness in her and an inability to enjoy anything real, even the weather—but then, as she says, you can make your own weather. You are your own companion, and there is no more fear, shame, or disappointment. Most of all, there is no responsibility to anyone. Mrs. Sammile's specialty is illusion, and she entices Pauline with it at their every meeting. She offers a place of quiet and solitude, where nothing changes and all of reality comes from within. Nothing from without can approach and frighten. For someone as fearful and somewhat closed off as Pauline there is temptation here. But Pauline is too far along the other path to listen very closely. Mrs. Sammile offers a life entirely of one's own making ("anything, everything, anything, everything" she repeats over and over), without a trace of trouble and without a trace of reality. It is entirely illusory, a fantasy, starting in the mind and taking on profound and lasting spiritual dimensions. "Take care of yourself. Think of yourself; be careful of yourself. I could make you perfectly safe and perfectly happy at the same time. . . . I could tell you tales that would shut everything but yourself out. . . . You'll never have to do anything for others any more."[34] Right up to the day of her final choice Pauline finds some appeal in this: "Pauline tingled as she listened. Shut up within herself— shut up till that very day with fear and duty for only companions . . . she felt a vague thrill of promised delight. Against it her release that day began already to seem provisional and weak."[35]

However, it is the words "You'll never have to do anything for others any more" that strike a note with Pauline that is so false it brings her back to reality. She turns her back on Mrs. Sammile, leaving her behind, "speaking hurriedly, wildly, and the voice rising on the wind and torn and flung on the wind: 'Anything, everything; anything everything; kindness to me . . . help to me . . . nothing to do for others, nothing to do with others . . . everything, everything . . .'"[36] To never have to do anything for anyone ever again and to concentrate on oneself. However, separated from God and others we are empty: a narcissism that ends in hell. In her final meeting with Lily Sammile, Pauline proclaims: "'How could I want anything but what is? . . . I only want everything to be as it is. . . . If it changes it shall change as it must, and I shall want it as it is then.' She laughed again at the useless attempt to explain."[37]

One would think that "choosing reality" is easy, even inevitable. It is not, particularly when we are increasingly surrounded by illusion in all forms of media. There is also denial of reality that is brought on by trauma, and that eventually must be faced for healing to take place. Choosing reality is often a courageous act, and God honors our efforts however small. When the One who is Himself the Truth leads us, all will be well. Sometimes Jesus takes us through dark places that require His healing touch so that we may be free to receive more of Him and live in His light and freedom as our true selves.

The generosity and openness of spirit that Williams advocates in *Descent into Hell* was apparently reflected in his own life. In the preface to *Essays Presented to Charles Williams* after his unexpected death at the age of forty-seven, C. S. Lewis had this to say about his dear friend: "The highest compliment I ever heard paid to them [Williams's manners] was by a nun. She said that Mr. Williams's manners implied a complete *offer* of intimacy without the slightest *imposition* of intimacy. He threw down all his own barriers without even implying that you should lower yours."[38] However, as is clear from his books, Charles Williams was a very complex man. Again, in the words of Lewis:

It is one of the many paradoxes in Williams that while no man's conversation was less gloomy in *tone*—it was, indeed, a continual flow of gaiety, enthusiasm, and high spirits—no man at times said darker things. He never forgot the infinite menaces of life, the unremitted possibility of torture, maiming, madness, bereavement, and (over all) that economic insecurity which, as he said in *War in Heaven,* poisons our sorrows as well as modifying our joys.

But that was only one side of him. This skepticism and pessimism were the expression of his feelings. High above them, overarching them like a sky, were the things he believed, and they were wholly optimistic. They did not negate the feelings: they mocked them. To the Williams who had accepted the fruition of Deity itself as the true goal of man, and who deeply believed that the sufferings of this present time were as nothing in comparison, the other Williams, the Williams who wished to be annihilated, who would rather not have been born, was in the last resort a comic figure.[39]

One is struck here by the enormity of Williams's fears and perhaps a level of safety in the arms of God that was not found or at least not expressed. Similarly, fear is a key theme in *Descent into Hell* and the hopeful outcome of Pauline's struggle is a testimony to Williams's belief rather than his feelings. Charles Williams's doctrine of substitution is not Christian. However, his understanding of the power of sacrificial love and its impact on the human race is a great gift to the reader. And his love of reality and of God's created world as displayed in *Descent into Hell* is inspiration to be courageous and to love it too.

Concluding Comments

On the six-month anniversary of the September 11 attack on America, I saw a documentary about some of the firefighters who went into the Twin Towers in New York City that day to try to save lives. A photographer, who had been following the lives of the firefighters in a firehouse near the World Trade Center, had accompanied them and filmed this historic event from their point of view inside the Towers. As I watched this remarkable video, I was struck by two things. First, the firefighters in the lobby of Tower One looked stunned and bewildered, and I realized that we who were watching everything unfold on television knew more than they did. I also saw fear in the eyes of some of these men. And then I saw them go into the stairwells, starting a climb of eighty flights. The fact that some of them were afraid and knew that they might not survive did not stop them from doing their job. The second thing that struck me was the story of the firefighter who remained at the bottom of a stairwell, directing those who emerged to the exit. By staying at this post he saved many lives, simply by saying "This way out" in the midst of total chaos. In fact, he sacrificed his life for what seems like a very simple act. As I observed this man's courage, I realized what a tremendous difference one person can make.

Courage does not have to do with the absence of fear. Rather, it means proceeding with a full knowledge of the evil or danger involved. Therefore, courage involves, more than anything else, vulnerability and trust in something greater than oneself. It also requires belief in a purpose and meaning to life that transcends the material world. A truly courageous act or attitude towards life requires a freedom from narcissism, the wrong kind of self-love. Perhaps more than anything else it is impossible to be courageous without a commitment to reality, however painful; all of the characters in this chapter have this in common. We have looked at three different expressions of courage: Elizabeth, who did not despise life in the face of disappointments; Betsey, who was willing to speak the truth when confronted with evil; and Pauline, who chose reality despite her fear.

There are so many others in literature who display different aspects of courage and who are worthy of imitation: Anne Shirley of *Anne of Green Gables,* who continues to hope and to believe in good and beautiful things despite the painful evidence of her life as an orphan; Melanie of *Gone with the Wind,* who lives according to a code of love and forgiveness and calls forth the good in everyone she encounters, even those who hate her; Meg of *A Wrinkle in Time,* who saves her little brother and herself from enslavement to evil when she realizes that love is the one thing that evil knows nothing about and cannot withstand; Jane of *That Hideous Strength,* who fears her own gifts and call and all that is transcendent but proceeds hesitantly forward until she meets God. These books, and countless others, are worth reading not once but many times.

Truly, courage has little to do with our own strength but with access to the strength of Another. Apparent weakness is really strength when we see the power of God manifested in the cross of Christ; here we see the power of love. It is the love relationship with God that casts out the fear in our souls. When we know that we are not alone in the universe but have a safe home with a loving Father, our fear is gone. We only gain true courage by letting Christ bear our burdens and fill us with His Spirit. In Him we have a refuge and a stronghold in this enemy territory where we are not only to follow His banner and do battle for Him but to be His ambassadors. Anyone can be a heroine when surrendered to a noble cause. For "God chose what is foolish in the world to shame the wise, God chose what is weak in the world to shame the strong" (1 Cor. 1:27).

Prayer

But we have this treasure in earthen vessels, to show that the transcendent power belongs to God and not to us. We are afflicted in every way, but not crushed; perplexed, but not driven to despair; persecuted but not forsaken; struck down, but not destroyed.

2 Corinthians 4:7–9

Dear Jesus,
Pour the love of God into my heart by the power of Your Holy Spirit, so that I might know what it is to be loved and cared for by the God of the universe. And may that love relationship cast out the fear in my heart.

Help me to acknowledge my weakness and total dependence on You for all things, that I may have a true source of strength and courage flowing through me.

Increase my faith so I do not fear the world so much that I fail to do what is right.

Open the eyes of my heart that I may rightly value the heroic acts and attitudes of others and seek to imitate them.

Give me discernment to recognize both good and evil, that I might love the one and hate the other. Please separate me from evil entirely, that You and You alone may reign in my heart.

Give me the grace to love reality, whatever my feelings may be. Lord, help me to know that I am not alone as I seek to face reality, including the pain of my own life, and help me to know too that You are the initiator of all healing, guiding and holding me. Help me to know in my head and heart that You have carried all my sin and suffering on the cross and have given me Your life in return. Help me to take my stand in Your death and resurrection.

Lord, give me opportunities to serve You and others sacrificially. Help me to imitate Your example of love. Amen.

4

The Wise Woman

Now faith is the assurance of things hoped for, the conviction of things not seen.

Hebrews 11:1

Courage and wisdom are similar in that both have to do with where—or in whom—we place our trust. Proverbs 28:26 states that "he who trusts in his own mind is a fool; but he who walks in wisdom will be delivered." Wisdom comes from God, and walking in wisdom is walking in His Spirit—the key to growth in the Christian life. Courage and wisdom also necessitate recognition of our own weakness and the need for strength and understanding outside of ourselves. It is out of love that God tells us in Psalm 111:10 that "the fear of the Lord is the beginning of wisdom," for He knows that He alone is trustworthy, and in Him we find our meaning and purpose. He knows that we would be desolate without Him. The fear of the Lord is an awareness of God, of the difference between the Creator and the created, and of the fact that without Him we cannot live. Perhaps more than any other, the process of seeking after wisdom highlights the key to acquiring any gift or virtue. In our longing for wisdom, our longing for God must come first. We are seeking the Giver, not the gift.

Paul's first letter to the Corinthians and the letter of James differentiate between wisdom from heaven or from God and the wisdom of the world or of men. These passages and others point to the results of seeking the wisdom that comes from above. Wisdom brings with it an understanding of the things of the Spirit of God, an apprehension of divine truth. Paul points to the example of the cross, which "is folly to those who are perishing, but to us who are being saved it is the power of God" (1 Cor. 1:18). Worldly wisdom might call the crucifixion a defeat instead of a victory. Yet the fruit of that "defeat" changed the history of the world. With wisdom we can apprehend the mystery of the cross, as well as perceive God in the midst of our own sufferings. In the Book of James we read, "Count it all joy, my brethren, when you meet various trials, for you know that the testing of your faith produces steadfastness. And let steadfastness have its full effect, that you may be perfect and complete, lacking in nothing. If any of you lacks wisdom, let him ask God, who gives to all men generously and without reproaching, and it will be given him" (1:2–5). The Spirit of God also gives us a glimpse of hope yet unseen but destined to be fulfilled by the God who always keeps His promises.

> None of the rulers of this age understood this; for if they had, they would not have crucified the Lord of glory. But, as it is written, "What no eye has seen, nor ear heard, nor the heart of man conceived, what God has prepared for those who love him," God has revealed to us through the Spirit.
>
> 1 Corinthians 2:8–10

In Proverbs wisdom is personified as a woman:

Does not wisdom call,
    does not understanding raise her voice?
On the heights beside the way,
    in the paths she takes her stand; . . .
for wisdom is better than jewels,
    and all that you may desire cannot compare with
    her. . . .
I have counsel and sound wisdom,
    I have insight, I have strength.

                                    Proverbs 8:1–2, 11, 14

We become mature by listening to God and receiving the Word He sends us. Much that is gained with wisdom is associated with the true feminine necessary for men and women alike. This true feminine holds the key to gaining wisdom—an attitude of receptivity. In the words of Leanne Payne:

> The essence of the true feminine is response to God, others, and all that *is*. As a quality in God, we all—men and women alike—are to participate in her and receive her capacity to say, with Mary, "Be it unto me according to Thy will." We then conceive within the womb of our spirits more of God and more of all that is true, beautiful, and good.
>
> In the story of Mary and Martha, Mary chose to sit receptively before the Lord. Hers was the true feminine response, which affirms and strengthens the true feminine within. We receive wisdom from God. Men are only healed in their true masculine—the power to initiate and to do the full will of God—as they are strengthened in their bridal identity. This is the power to respond and be penctrated, through and through, with the fear of the Lord—the fear of a masculine that is so powerful that we are all feminine in relation to it.[1]

The wisdom from above is pure and complete, and it is more important to trust and to patiently wait on God than to overanalyze or second-guess His Word. It is also important to not diminish the wisdom given or "dumb it down" out of a sense of personal inadequacy or doubt about the ability of others to receive what God has to give. This might be a tendency of some women who are taught to subjugate themselves to others rather than serve God alone, or to embrace the mediocre rather than the full gift of God. It is a remarkable fact that God reveals Himself to us by His Spirit. This can be difficult to accept: God calls us to great things as we mature in Him.

The wisdom of God is powerful. It can simplify a complicated situation or provide an answer to a stubborn question. It provides the understanding necessary to govern nations. It gives us the ability to see something for what it truly is and to find the good in a difficult situation. Thus we grow in objective reality—the ability to stand back and see the activity of God rather than being overcome by painful emotions. This can present a challenge for women who are so attuned to the feeling being.

The wise actions of the women in this chapter are based on trust in God, whether an intuitive, childlike trust, a bold, risky trust, or a small but determined step in God's direction. All of these are honored by the One who loves a trusting heart and is moved by belief in Him.

Psyche in *Till We Have Faces*
C. S. Lewis

> Whoever seeks to gain his life will lose it, but whoever loses his life will preserve it.
>
> Luke 17:33

Nowhere does C. S. Lewis speak of the glories and mysteries of human destiny as powerfully as in his retelling of the Cupid and Psyche myth in his 1956 novel, *Till We Have Faces*. Here we see a series of characters each coated with varying layers of self-deception and scars of pain untouched through long years. In this story the degree to which the true self may be realized and God may be known depends upon the wisdom gained by two complementary roads: imagination that is sanctified to see beyond the limits of earthly reality and the wounds of sin and evil, and courage that makes it possible to face the truth about oneself beyond the limits of self-deception and self-pity. These are the seeds of godly glory implanted by God Himself in every human being and drawn out, either slowly or dramatically, in preparation for the eternal realms.

In the original tale of Cupid and Psyche, Psyche is the youngest and most beautiful of three sisters who inspires the rage and jealousy of Venus when people begin to look upon her as a goddess. As a result Venus arranges for Psyche to be sacrificed to the god of the Mountain who is thought to be a hideous monster, but she is taken instead at the last moment by Venus's son, Cupid, to his palace to be his bride. Lewis alters the story by Apuleius in such a way as to emphasize the nature of God, the nature of humanity, and the relationship between the two. He presents six main characters displaying differing perceptions of themselves, others, and God. As in all fairy tales, there is the Sudden Joyous Turn (a term used by J. R. R. Tolkien) as humility follows pride, confession and forgiveness follow sin, and life follows death. Imagination is released to usher in hope for a different destiny, and fear of the truth is replaced by courage to know both self and God.

In Lewis's *The Great Divorce* cases of dramatic disintegration of the soul are given the opportunity for painful remedy as essential preparation for eternity. So Lewis puts forth the theory that, even in the midst of sin, there is a core of longing for God within each individual, and the painful job of digging it out, for which human beings possess neither the desire nor the ability, lies in divine hands.

In *Till We Have Faces* the distance from the core is shorter for Psyche than for the other characters. When she discovers that she is to be sacrificed to the god of the Mountain she is not filled with horror and fear as is her half-sister, Orual. This is because she does not believe that the mystery surrounding this god necessarily implies something evil. On the contrary, from her childhood she possessed an instinctive knowledge that the Mountain represented something of great beauty and solidity such as one could never find on earth.

"Orual," she said, her eyes shining, "I am going, you see, to the Mountain. You remember how we used to look and long? And all the stories of my gold and amber house, up there against the sky, where we thought we should never really go? The greatest King of all was going to build it for me. . . . The sweetest thing in all my life has been the longing—to reach the Mountain, to find the place where all the beauty came from . . . my country, the place where I ought to have been born. Do you think it all meant nothing, all the longing? The longing for home? For indeed it now feels not like going, but like going back. All my life the god of the Mountain has been wooing me. . . . I am going to my lover."[2]

How is it that Psyche is able to perceive with an astuteness unequaled by any other character in the novel that the Mountain may just possibly be other than barren and desolate and the god that lives there other than spiteful, merciless, and malevolent? Early in the story when she is still a child Psyche is often described as being "according to nature; what every woman, or even every thing, ought to have been and meant to be, but missed by some trip of chance."[3]

From Psyche's life we can deduce that this degree of "wholeness" is connected to certain characteristics. Her imagination seems to have been invaded and indeed sanctified by an objective spiritual force that allows her to envision and believe in things that are invisible to human eyes, outside of her experience, and not obviously attested to by the world around her. She does not believe that the death of the body is a terrible thing but only a door into a world for which she longs. Therefore, she possesses what those around her might see as extraordinary courage (or ignorance) to face the unknown, the mystery of the terrible god who will consume her. Psyche, however, does not see this as courage but as a completely natural decision born out of a true sense of who God is and who she is to Him. She has not been deceived or deceived herself about these things; she has wisdom.

There is then a type of courage born out of self-understanding that makes potentially difficult decisions absolutely clear and indeed inevitable. Later in the story Psyche must call upon another type of courage when after betraying the god she loves she must persevere to find him (and herself) again. There are others in the story, however, and most particularly Orual, who must know for the first time the pain, the grace, and the glory of facing who they really are and who God really is.

Till We Have Faces is narrated by Orual, the most complex of the six characters, and the book is really her story more than anyone else's. In fact, she tells us on the first page that we are about to read her accusation of the gods and especially the god of the Mountain who took Psyche from her. Orual accuses the gods because her life has been so filled with pain. Her physical ugliness, bestowed upon her by the gods, is referred to constantly throughout the book. She is abused both verbally and physically by her father until his death frees her. The one person who gave her happiness and love is Psyche, who is taken from her by the gods. When she finds Psyche alive on the Mountain she finds a Psyche apparently bewitched, whose primary loyalty is no longer to Orual but to the god of the Mountain who is also her husband. Orual sees this as a betrayal and a madness from which she must save her sister. So Orual threatens to kill herself if Psyche does not betray the god who has commanded her not to look upon him by lighting a lamp in the darkness when they are together. Orual believes this to be a true test of Psyche's love for her. In reality, however, it is only the mark of her craving for Psyche, her desire to possess her and to be needed and loved by her—whatever the cost to Psyche.

Orual is brave yet cowardly, strong yet weak, loving yet filled with bitterness. She is running from herself and from the gods. She ignores the truth until it catches up with her and relies on her own wisdom. She is selfish and jealous. She lives off other human beings, thinking she is generous of spirit and perceptive of mind, yet she is actually oblivious to the needs and true natures of those around her.

In the end Orual sees her true face; she has been the jealous and consuming god of her people (Ungit), and she will be Psyche through the purging of her lifelong self-deception and bitterness. While the true god remained hidden from her understanding until she should have eyes to see and ears to hear him, she made the gods in her own ugly image, perhaps to absolve herself from blame. She blames the gods for remaining invisible to her; what could she do but assume that her sister is mad and drag her away from the paradise that Psyche can see with the eyes of faith and trust? But Orual does see Psyche's palace on the Mountain—very clearly in fact, although it does not last. She chooses to believe this was not a true vision and blames the gods for not speaking more plainly to her if they wanted her to believe in its existence. The truth is more likely that such a vision did not suit her ultimate purpose, which was to make Psyche her own again.

At the moment of Psyche's betrayal of the god, Orual herself meets him face to face:

> A monster . . . would have subdued me less than the beauty this face wore. . . . He rejected, denied, answered, and (worst of all) knew, all that I had thought, done or been. . . . He made it to be as if, from the beginning, I had known that Psyche's lover was a god, and as if all

125

my doubtings, fears, guessings, debatings, questionings of Bardia, questionings of the Fox, all the rummage of business of it, had been trumped up foolery, dust blown in my own eyes by myself.[4]

At this point Orual is convinced that the gods exist and that they hate her and wish to punish her. It is not until the very end of her life that she begins to see that she used those around her for her own purposes out of self-pity and self-deception. In the final days of her life she is given a vision that opens her hardened heart and reveals to her the reality of what she might have imagined—the unseen world and the true nature of the gods. When she meets the real God He is nothing like what she expected or feared or did not believe in. The most amazing thing of all is that He loved her enough all along to desire her to be as beautiful, as whole, and as close to Himself as Psyche.

> If Psyche had not held me by the hand I should have sunk down. She had brought me now to the very edge of the pool. The air was growing brighter and brighter around us; as if something had set it on fire. Each breath I drew let me into new terror, joy, overpowering sweetness. I was pierced through and through with the arrows of it. I was being unmade. I was no one. But that's little to say; rather Psyche herself was, in a manner, no one. I loved her as I would once have thought it impossible to love, would have died any death for her. And yet it was not, not now, she that really counted. Or if she counted (and oh, gloriously she did) it was for another's sake. The earth and stars and sun, all that was or will be, existed for his sake. And he was coming. The most dreadful, the most beautiful, the only dread and beauty there is, was coming. The pillars on the far side of the pool flushed with his approach. I cast down my eyes.

Two figures, reflections, their feet to Psyche's feet and mine, stood head downward in the water. But whose were they? Two Psyches, the one clothed, the other naked? Yes, both Psyches, both beautiful (if that mattered now) beyond all imagining, yet not exactly the same.

"You also are Psyche," came a great voice.[5]

Not only was God too terrible and too beautiful to admit into her life, but the "weight of glory" referred to by C. S. Lewis that was truly hers to bear was not at all what she thought it meant to be Orual. Ultimately what it means to be gloriously human is to share in the divine life through the Savior of our souls. We too can be sanctified until we bear the image of Psyche—courageous, trusting, and given grace to see a clear and beautiful image in the mirror of our souls, to know God and to long for Him. When we are ready to receive from God we receive wisdom to see the truth about ourselves rather than the lies we tell ourselves or the lies we have heard from others and taken in as truth. There are no ordinary people. Orual concludes with these words: "I know now, Lord, why you utter no answer. You yourself are the answer. Before your face questions die away."[6]

Celia in The Cocktail Party

T. S. Eliot

I saw today that there was one thing unforgivable—like things in the school-room, so bad they were unpunishable, that only mummy could deal with—the bad thing I was on the point of doing, that I'm not quite bad enough to do; to set up a rival good to God's.

Evelyn Waugh[7]

Perhaps that's just part of my illness,
But I feel it would be a kind of surrender—
No, not a surrender—more like a betrayal.
You see, I think I really had a vision of something
Though I don't know what it is. I don't want to
    forget it.
I want to live with it. I could do without every-
    thing,
Put up with anything, if I might cherish it.

T. S. Eliot[8]

In our unguarded moments, what sort of Person do we imagine God to be? Do we project human failings onto Him, seeing Him as remote, demanding, or even passive? Do we know for certain that God is the least passive being one could ever imagine, that He is the essence of initiation, creativity, and action? He is the One who seeks us, hears us, sees us, and loves us. Both the Old and the New Testaments of the Bible tell us plainly who God really is. Indeed, the whole of the Old Testament is the story of a relationship that is continually broken and restored. Only God is faithful and consistent, calling the people He loves back to Himself, seeing and hearing all they do and revealing Himself to them. In the New Testament we meet the One who is Himself "the image of the invisible God" (Col. 1:15). In the fifteenth chapter of the Gospel of Luke Jesus tells two stories of how His Father sees those who are lost—the lost sheep and the lost son.

The God who hears, who sees, and who seeks is also always speaking. He is calling to us; do we hear His voice? Can we receive our call? Do we respond to the voice of God? Our wisdom lies in the desire and the increasing ability to hear and respond to the wisdom from above. The responses to God of the women in this section, even with trepidation, are the essence of wisdom. There is a strong sense of "Let it be to me according to your word" (Luke 1:38). Celia of T. S. Eliot's (1888–1965) play *The Cocktail Party* and Julia of Evelyn Waugh's (1903–1966) novel *Brideshead Revisited* choose what may seem to be a very lonely path in life. Yet nothing could be further from the truth. They are rejecting the ultimate separation from God that would be characterized by unendurable isolation for any human soul. In the words of Mother Teresa, "The greatest disease in the world is not starvation, it's loneliness." Moreover, I have rarely read anything that so completely dispelled that sense of solitude and even "homesickness" (unrelated to the loving presence of friends and family) as in certain sections of these two works.

They capture the wind of the Spirit that blows through the soul, saying to every individual, "Come home! Come home!"

At this moment, as I look out my window, a high wind is blowing in the trees, and a bird is simply floating up and down, backwards and forwards, on the wind. Answering the call of God to come home looks a little like this. It is relaxing into the wind of the Spirit and receiving its direction in trust.

The human need to belong, to have a place in the world, is profound. In Christ we do have a place and a loving Father; we are not orphans. Jesus said: "Let not your hearts be troubled. . . . In my Father's house are many rooms; if it were not so, would I have told you that I go to prepare a place for you? . . . If a man loves me, he will keep my word, and my Father will love him, and we will come to him and make our home with him" (John 14:1–2, 23). God knows our need for home better than we do. He knows that we need the constant companionship of the lover of our souls. My own faith began when I was a small child; I knew someone walked with me all the time and was with me when I went to bed at night. I knew it was the person called Jesus, who was in a picture that hung in our hallway with the "Our Father" written below it and also on the crucifix in my parents' bedroom. I always knew that I could talk to this comforting person.

No place or person on earth can meet the deepest needs of the soul as God can. There is a difference between the normal human need for love and companionship and the need for someone to give meaning and purpose. No human being is worthy of worship or capable of forgiving sin. That is the difference Celia and Julia encounter, initially much to their distress and confusion. The voice they hear is so irresistible that they turn their backs on the most precious treasures this world has to offer, treasures that are readily at their disposal. The paths they choose are not for everyone; for some, following that still, small voice may mean staying in a relationship rather than leaving, or serving those who are difficult to love in one's own family circle. However, both Celia and Julia are in situations that require a radical change in lifestyle to answer that still, small voice.

Celia, a young socialite from a wealthy background, has two men in love with her at the beginning of the play. She describes her upbringing as:

> pretty conventional—
> I had always been taught to disbelieve in sin.
> Oh, I don't mean that it was ever mentioned!
> But anything wrong, from our point of view,
> Was either bad form, or was psychological."[9]

But when Edward, the man she loves (or thinks she loves) rejects her in favor of returning to his wife, Lavinia, her real needs quickly surface. Believing she is ill, she visits Dr. Harcourt-Reilly, also known as the "Uninvited Guest" who appears throughout the play. He is a therapist who sees into the souls of his patients and determines their real need. At this point, Celia is not practicing any self-deception. She is honest with herself and Dr. Reilly but is nonetheless convinced she has an illness; her symptoms are at one and the same time so unmentionable and so unmistakable.

Celia: Well, there are two things I can't understand,
   Which you might consider symptoms. But first
      I must tell you
   That I should really *like* to think there's something wrong with me—

Because, if there isn't, then there's something
    wrong,
Or at least, very different from what it seemed
    to be,
With the world itself—and that's much more
    frightening!
That would be terrible. So I'd rather believe
There is something wrong with me, that could
    be put right.
I'd do anything you told me, to get back to nor-
    mality.

Reilly: We must find out about you, before we decide
What *is* normality. You say there are two
    things:
What is the first?

Celia: An awareness of solitude . . .
I mean that what has happened has made me
    aware
That I've always been alone. That one is always
    alone
No . . . it isn't that I *want* to be alone,
But that everyone's alone—or so it seems to me.
They make noises, and think they are talking to
    each other;
They make faces, and think they understand
    each other.
And I'm sure they don't. Is that a delusion?

Reilly: A delusion is something we must return from.
There are other states of mind, which we take
    to be delusion,
But which we have to accept and go on from.
And the second symptom?

Celia: That's stranger still.
It sounds ridiculous—but the only word for it
That I can find, is a sense of sin.

Reilly: You suffer from a sense of sin, Miss Coplestone?
This is most unusual . . .

Celia: It's not the feeling of anything I've ever *done*,
      Which I might get away from, or of anything in
        me
      I could get rid of—but of emptiness, of failure
      Towards someone, or something, outside
        myself;
      And I feel I must . . . *atone*—is that the word?
      Can you treat a patient for such a state of
        mind?[10]

Celia is blessed: she has not only experienced that primal solitude that is the lot of every human being, but she has had a glimpse of its cure. She speaks of searching for a treasure, although she is not certain that it can ever be found. She sought that treasure in her relationship with Edward but could not find it there. Now that she has seen the solitude and sin beneath her pain over Edward's rejection of her, she has only compassion for him. Still, she is left with an even greater longing for that treasure.

      But even if I find my way out of the forest
      I shall be left with the inconsolable memory
      Of the treasure I went into the forest to find
      And never found, and which was not there
      And perhaps is not anywhere? But if not any-
        where,
      Why do I feel guilty at not having found it? . . .
      For what happened is remembered like a
        dream
      In which one is exalted by intensity of loving
      In the spirit, a vibration of delight
      Without desire, for desire is fulfilled
      In the delight of loving. A state one does not
        know
      When awake. But what, or whom I loved,
      Or what in me was loving, I do not know.
      And if that is all meaningless, I want to be
        cured

Of a craving for something I cannot find
And of the shame of never finding it.
Can you cure me?[11]

Celia feels that she has had a vision of something or someone to love, and she would sacrifice everything to cherish it.

I couldn't give anyone the kind of love—
I wish I could—which belongs to that life.
Oh, I'm afraid this sounds like raving!
Or just cantankerousness . . . still,
If there's no other way . . . then I just feel hope-
    less.[12]

Reilly tells Celia that her condition is curable, but that she must choose her form of treatment. The treatment is different for everyone, depending on their condition. For instance, Edward must practice a sacrificial love for his wife and forget himself. Reilly sends his patients away with the same parting words for each: "Go in peace. And work out your salvation with diligence."[13] And the theme is always the same: "If you lose your life for my sake, you will find it." Celia's choice is a radical one. She cannot betray the vision she had; she embarks on the road towards it and turns her back on the world she has known but in which she never really found her home.

Reilly: There *is* another way, if you have the courage.
        The first I could describe in familiar terms
        Because you have seen it, as we all have seen it,
        Illustrated, more or less, in lives of those about
            us.
        The second is unknown, and so requires faith—
        The kind of faith that issues from despair.
        The destination cannot be described;

134

You will know very little until you get there;
You will journey blind. But the way leads
   towards possession
Of what you have sought for in the wrong
   place.

Celia: That sounds like what I want. But what is my
   duty?

Reilly: Whichever way you choose will prescribe its own
   duty.

Celia: Which way is better?

Reilly: Neither way is better.
   Both ways are necessary. It is also necessary
   To make a choice between them.

Celia: Then I choose the second.

Reilly: It is a terrifying journey.

Celia: I am not frightened
   But glad.[14]

When Celia leaves Dr. Reilly's office neither he nor she knows exactly where her choice will lead her. She goes to his "sanitorium," presumably to spend time listening to the voice of God, focusing her eyes on the glimpse of love given to her. In the final act of the play we discover that she went to a remote part of Africa as a missionary nurse and was martyred there. She could have left but would not abandon the sick African natives in her care. It is a shocking ending, but at the same time the sense that she has fulfilled her calling is powerful. And the contrast between the setting of a London cocktail party and the news of Celia's death shared there is offset by the new unity and genuine caring found among the other guests, and especially between Edward and Lavinia, who were so divided in Act I. Everyone had choices to make; Celia's choice was not "better" than

Edward's and Lavinia's, just different. All three took the road of service and self-forgetfulness.

From the beginning of the play there is a vulnerability about Celia that becomes more pronounced after Edward rejects her. She has been brought up to ignore God and her conscience, but she is by no means a hardened atheist. Her visit with Dr. Reilly seems like an event waiting to happen; it is not a matter of a veneer or worldly sophistication falling away or defenses breaking down. They are simply nonexistent at this point, and she enters the doctor's office ready to change her life; she only needs direction. It happened to be the end of her relationship with Edward that precipitated this; it could have been anything.

Julia in Brideshead Revisited
Evelyn Waugh

The Only Cure for Sin and Sadness

Julia, of *Brideshead Revisited*, on the other hand, undergoes a clearly observable transformation on spiritual, emotional, and even physical levels. She holds on to her hopes of a life without God up until the closing chapters of the novel. Long before this, however, her transformation begins. When Charles Ryder, the narrator of the story, first encounters Julia, the sister of his best friend, Sebastian, the reader receives a general impression of a partly assumed hardness in her. It is real enough, but one cannot help feeling that she is deceiving herself, that she is pretending on some level to be something she is not.

> "I must say it's noble of you to come all this way at a moment's notice." But as she said it, I heard, or thought I heard, a tiny note of contempt in her voice that I should be so readily available. . . .
>
> Her dark hair was scarcely longer than Sebastian's, and it blew back from her forehead as his did; her eyes on the darkling road were his, but larger; her painted mouth was less friendly to the world.[15]

137

Years later, Charles meets Julia unexpectedly aboard ship en route from America to England. She has changed:

> There was nothing but humility and friendly candour in the way she spoke. . . .
> "You have [changed], Charles. So lean and grim; not at all the pretty boy Sebastian brought home with him. Harder, too."
> "And you're softer."
> "Yes, I think so . . . and very patient now."
> She was not yet thirty, but was approaching the zenith of her loveliness, all her rich promise abundantly fulfilled. . . .
> Time had wrought another change, too; not for her the sly, complacent smile of la Gioconda; the years had been more than "the sounds of lyres and flutes," and had saddened her.
> That was the change in her from ten years ago; that, indeed, was her reward, this haunting, magical sadness which spoke straight to the heart and struck silence; it was the completion of her beauty.
> "Sadder, too," I said.
> "Oh yes, much sadder."[16]

Julia already embodies an important part of the true feminine in that she describes herself as "very patient now." No longer driven by the need to make a good English society marriage despite her Catholicism, she has developed more of the capacity *to be,* and this only heightens her attractiveness as a woman. Her personal transformation seems to reflect the change in the times both symbolically and in the fact that she has left the frantic pace of the 1920s behind and is preparing for the impending crisis in the world and in her own soul. Her capacity to be is the key to receiving the wisdom from above. She is open to receiving love from

Charles, but her softened heart is now also preparing to receive God. Thus her emotional and physical transformation, partly the result of suffering through ten years in an unhappy marriage with a cold and faithless husband and a miscarriage, is observed by Charles. However, he begins to glimpse a spiritual awakening in her sadness, not suspecting that this will one day draw her loyalty away from him and towards God.

And it came back to me that this was how she had sat in the liner, before the storm; this was how she had looked, and I realized that she had regained what I thought she had lost forever, the magical sadness which had drawn me to her, the thwarted look that had seemed to say, "Surely I was made for some other purpose than this?" . . .

And another image came to me, of an arctic hut and a trapper alone with his furs and oil lamp and log fire; everything dry and ship-shape and warm inside, and outside the last blizzard of the winter raging and the snow piling up against the door. Quite silently a great weight forming against the timber; the bolt straining in its socket; minute by minute in the darkness outside the white heap sealing the door, until quite soon when the wind dropped and the sun came out on the ice slopes and the thaw set in a block would move, slide, and tumble, high above, gather weight, till the whole hillside seemed to be falling, and the little lighted place would open and splinter and disappear, rolling with the avalanche into the ravine.[17]

Charles and Julia do fall in love on board ship and abandon their spouses. They are together for two years until Julia's brother, Brideshead, refers to her relationship with Charles as "living in sin." Charles is furious with Brideshead:

"Bridey, what a bloody offensive thing to say to Julia!"
"There was nothing she should object to. I was merely stating a fact well known to her."[18]

Brideshead is pompous and unkind, but he has stated a fact. Julia is immediately overwhelmed by the name given not only to her actions but to her life. Charles follows her out onto the grounds of the estate, where he finds her sobbing. She pours out her grief over her own sin that she now sees not only as fact but as inescapable fact because she has turned her back on God.

> *"Living in sin,"* with sin, always the same, like an idiot child carefully nursed, guarded from the world. "Poor Julia," they say, "she can't go out. She's got to take care of her sin. A pity it ever lived," they say, "but it's so strong. Children like that always are. Julia's so good to her little, mad sin." . . .
>
> A word from so long ago; from Nanny Hawkins stitching by the hearth and the nightlight burning before the Sacred Heart . . . mummy dying with my sin eating at her, more cruelly than her own deadly illness.
>
> Mummy dying with it; Christ dying with it, nailed hand and foot; hanging over the bed in the night-nursery; hanging year after year in the dark little study at Farm Street with the shining oilcloth; hanging in the dark church where only the old charwoman raises the dust and one candle burns; hanging at noon, high among the crowds and the soldiers; no comfort except a sponge of vinegar and the kind words of a thief; hanging forever; never the cool sepulchre and the grave clothes spread on the stone slab, never the oil and spices in the dark cave; always the midday sun and the dice clicking for the seamless coat.[19]

The acute awareness of her sin, of God carrying her sin, and of her separation from God and her need of God make her feel as if she is going crazy. "Charles, am I going crazy? What's happened tonight? I'm so tired . . . tired and crazy and good for nothing."[20] But she is not crazy. On the contrary, she is crashing headlong into reality.

The heart of *Brideshead Revisited* is not any single character but faith itself—that faith that rises to the surface again and again, like the waves that literally throw Charles and Julia together on the ship; that faith that falls like an avalanche over the lives of Charles and Julia, sweeping them with it; the faith that spans the centuries and ultimately cannot be ignored, even by atheist Charles. The period of suffering that Julia endures opens her heart to human frailty, including her own, but it is her relationship with Charles and then the death of her father that precipitate the central spiritual crisis of her life. While Celia has been brought up to ignore God and her conscience, Julia has been brought up to believe in God and to take Him seriously.

As in so many stories and real-life situations, there is a difference between the real God and His irresistible draw and the real faith—as they truly are, which are at the center of this story—and how He is presented through human failings and dismissed for these reasons. There is a real faith in a real God in the hearts of this family, despite their sin and weakness, and they cling to it. Even if they do not entirely understand the grace and gentle, loving heart of God, He is calling to them ceaselessly. The objective fact of Christianity transcends all human failing and presentation. It is bigger than all of that.

Lord and Lady Marchmain have brought up three children who desperately need the true God of love and mercy. The youngest daughter, Cordelia, always knows Him and remains close to His heart. In the final chapters of the book we see the three most unlikely members of the family return to the faith, and they are perhaps closer to the truth of grace in Christ than Lady Marchmain and her older son, Brideshead. Neither Sebastian, Julia, nor their father ultimately can forget something that has been true for thousands of years, something that tugs at each individual heart. Sebastian wanders the world, looking to fill the needs of his soul with alcohol and other destructive means. Finally, he arrives at the doors of a Tibetan monastery and spends his last days there in the care of the monks. Lord Marchmain comes home to die and begins to recognize his sin, asking Cordelia if his desertion of her mother was a crime:

> "Then I went away—left her in the chapel praying. It was hers. It was the place for her. I never came back to disturb her prayers. They said we were fighting for freedom; I had my own victory. Was it a crime?"
> "I think it was, papa."[21]

It is her father's death that makes Julia finally realize she can no more do without God than he can. There is a conflict between Julia and Charles over whether her father should see a priest in his dying moments, and it highlights once again that the stirrings of Julia's soul have placed her at a distance from the self-proclaimed atheist she loves. One receives the impression that this time it is Charles who is desperately holding on to his disbelief.

> "I really can't see why you've taken it so much to heart that my father shall not have the last sacraments."
> "It's such a lot of witchcraft and hypocrisy."
> "Is it? Anyway, it's been going on for nearly two thousand years. I don't know why you should suddenly get in a rage now." . . .

I knew these fierce moods of Julia's, such as had over-
taken her at the fountain in moonlight, and dimly sur-
mised their origin; I knew they could not be assuaged
by words. Nor could I have spoken, for the answer to
her question was still unformed; the sense that the fate
of more souls than one was at issue; that the snow was
beginning to shift on the high slopes.[22]

Initially Lord Marchmain rejects the priest's visit, and
Charles is triumphant:

I carried the news to Julia, who lay with her bed-table
amid a litter of newspapers and envelopes. "Mumbo-
jumbo is off," I said. "The witch-doctor is gone."
"Poor papa."
"It's great sucks to Bridey."
I felt triumphant. I had been right, everyone else had
been wrong, truth had prevailed; the threat that I had
felt hanging over Julia and me ever since that evening
at the fountain, had been averted, perhaps dispelled for
ever.[23]

However, the priest visits again, and Lord Marchmain
in his dying moments does ask and receive forgiveness
from God for his sins. Both Charles and Julia are there
to see it. This time Charles speaks to the God he does
not believe in:

"O God, if there is a God, forgive him his sins, if there
is such a thing as sin." . . . I suddenly felt the longing for
a sign, if only of courtesy, if only for the sake of the
woman I loved, who knelt in front of me, praying, I
knew, for a sign. . . . I prayed more simply; "God, forgive him his sins" and "Please God, make him accept
your forgiveness." . . .
Suddenly Lord Marchmain moved his hand to his
forehead . . . the hand moved slowly down his breast,
then to his shoulder, and Lord Marchmain made the

sign of the cross. Then I knew that the sign I had asked for was not a little thing, not a passing nod of recognition, and a phrase came back to me from my childhood of the veil of the temple being rent from top to bottom.[24]

Julia and Charles's relationship ends here. But a relationship with God begins for both of them. In Julia's words:

The worse I am, the more I need God. I can't shut myself out from his mercy. That is what it would mean; starting a life with you, without him. One can only hope to see one step ahead. But I saw today that there was one thing unforgivable—like things in the school-room, so bad they were unpunishable, that only mummy could deal with—the bad thing I was on the point of doing, that I'm not quite bad enough to do; to set up a rival good to God's. Why should I be allowed to understand that, and not you, Charles?[25]

Charles tells Julia that he does understand, and by the last page of the book we know that this is true. All of this story is told by Charles as a flashback, and the last chapter brings us up-to-date—a few years later and to World War II, when Charles finds himself stationed back at Brideshead setting up a temporary army camp. While there, he discovers that Julia is overseas serving as a nurse with her sister. In the final scene he pays a visit to the old chapel, where he finds the same lamp burning.

I said a prayer, an ancient, newly-learned form of words, and left, turning towards the camp; and as I walked back, and the cook-house bugle sounded ahead of me, I thought:
"Something quite remote from anything the builders intended, has come out of their work, and out of the

fierce little human tragedy in which I played; something none of us thought about at the time; a small red flame— a beaten-copper lamp of deplorable design relit before the beaten-copper doors of a tabernacle; the flame which the old knights saw from their tombs, which they saw put out; that flame burns again for other soldiers, far from home, farther, in heart, than Acre or Jerusalem. It could not have been lit but for the builders and tragedians, and there I found it this morning, burning anew among the old stones."

I quickened my pace and reached the hut which served us for our ante-room.

"You're looking unusually cheerful today," said the second-in-command.[26]

A Madame Curie may develop what one commonly considers as male gifts, i.e. talents in the field of the analytic-scientific; and preserve the womanly core of her nature. Women in holy orders, such as Saint Teresa of Avila or Mother Cabrini, have often displayed a physical tenacity, a fighting spirit, a sense of practical affairs worthy of a male "executive type"—and yet that certain sense of the womanly is invariably there, in between the lines as it were. Under pioneer conditions women clear forests, dig wells and build houses—and their femininity persists underneath it like a permanent foundation. Saint Catherine of Siena exhorted, prophetically, the Pope; Saint Joan of Arc rode at the head of an army. I, for one, in reading their life histories never lose the sense of womanliness.[27]

The woman of wisdom focuses our attention on the essence of the true feminine. It is therefore an appropriate time to emphasize that the *true* feminine has little to do with either of the stereotypes of femininity found in the world and, I am afraid, even in the church—a woman pictured as either mild, passive, silent, and perhaps not very intelligent, or manipulative, cunning, petulant, and insincere. Nor is she the extreme feminist image—aggressive and competitive with a thinly veiled attitude of mockery and even disgust towards men. It is possible to be a traditional woman in home and church and not be the least bit feminine; it is equally possible to have a nontraditional role such as those mentioned above and be extremely feminine. "If things are right, her womanliness helps her to develop her creativeness in whatever work she has chosen."[28]

It is equally important for both men and women to embrace the true feminine in order to be healthy. In his brilliant book *The Flight from Woman* Karl Stern discusses the true feminine at length and in the context of certain great philosophers and writers. His premise is that both men and women have run from the true feminine and are left bereft and neurotic, without the ability to receive love, to be actively passive, to intuit, wait, know, and be, to accept a healthy dependence and need. (Joan of Arc rode at the head of an army, but she received her vision from God and recognized her dependence on Him. Madame Curie was a scientist, but she also relied on intuition, had faith in what she could not see against all odds, and had a vibrant partnership with her husband that inspired her.) These characteristics are crucial to our relationship with God if we are to receive our calling and live for Him; they are also crucial to healthy relationships between human beings.

In the Book of Proverbs, Wisdom is practically begging the reader to receive. She cries, Do not turn away from me, do not fly from me! This is like the voice of God calling to us, where He is the Bridegroom and His people are the bride. In this sense, as mentioned earlier, we are all feminine in our response to God. We cannot be whole without the vulnerability, trust, and the generous and open spirit that are part of the true feminine. Karl Stern refers to woman not as "irrational" but as "trans-rational":

> Perhaps the most felicitous expression was found by Ortega y Gasset: "The more of a man one is, the more he is filled to the brim with rationality. Everything he does and achieves, he does and achieves for a reason, especially for a practical reason. A woman's love, that

divine surrender of her ultra-inner being which the impassioned woman makes, is perhaps the only thing which is not achieved by reasoning. The core of the feminine mind, no matter how intelligent the woman may be, is occupied by an irrational power. If the male is the rational being, the woman is the irrational being." The word "irrational" does not go well in this context since in English it often has the connotation of "foolish" or "stupid." There should be another word, such as "trans-rational," because Ortega, just as Helene Deutsch and others, speaks of a form of *knowledge* or *awareness* which is not only independent of reason but goes *beyond* it. . . . Hence, woman's "strength is the intuitive grasp of the living concrete; especially of the personal element. She has the special gift of making herself at home in the inner world of others." When Ortega states that a woman's love is "perhaps the only thing which is not achieved by reasoning," we are reminded of Dante's statement about women "who possess the spirit of love" *('ch'avete intelletto d'amore').*[29]

The knowledge or awareness that goes beyond reason is essential for anyone, both men and women, in order to intuit the divine. Celia and Julia have what may certainly be called "trans-rational" experiences when they hear the call of God and respond to it. The true feminine is not to be feared and flown from, and the denial of it leaves both men and women half of what they were intended to be. An example of this may be found in Karl Stern's remarkable assessment of the effects of the break in Tolstoy's marriage and his rejection of the church on his life and writing. Here we see that "the mystery of the womanly is bound up with the mystery of the supernatural life."[30] Indeed, we find here such a powerful example of some of the themes of our discussion that it is worth devoting the final paragraphs of this chapter to Stern's summary of Tolstoy and Sonya and the church.

When Tolstoy experienced his "conversion" he embraced a purely moralistic Christianity that he believed was based on the pure gospel but with no supernatural element. Dostoyevsky called it a "religion without sky."[31]

> When one reads the story of Tolstoy's conversion in all its phases, with the eventual doubt of the incarnation and of the sacramental in the life of the Church, of the destruction of the faith of his childhood, that entire *denial of the sensory*—there is no doubt about it: what he was converted to was a position of *dis*trust.
>
> Loving abandon is not only a constituent of Christian faith but also a constituent of Christian morals, for morals cannot be separated from faith. If morality is divorced from faith, it regresses and becomes a juggernaut driven by explosive fuel. When, after Tolstoy's conversion, his marriage had developed into a focus of hate, the poor Countess confided to her diary that *before* his conversion they had had more Christianity. And she was right, of course.[32]

The effect of his rejection of the incarnation and his hatred of his wife was catastrophic for his writing. His genius, separated from the true feminine found in both his wife and the church, produced none of the integrated beauty, the balance of objective truth and genuine feeling found in *Anna Karenin* and *War and Peace*. He took to producing pamphlets on moral teaching.

> When Tolstoy writes only for the sake of poetry, completely devoid of the tendentious, one page on the most trivial everyday scene reveals more of the eternal spirit than all his pamphlets on religion put together. . . . Once he announced to [Sonya] in a letter from Moscow that

a purely narrative idea had come to him, and she answered: "What joy I felt, when I read that you again feel an impulse to write in a poetical vein. That is what I have so long hoped and waited for. In that lies your salvation and happiness. . . . This is the kind of work for which you were created. Without it there can never be any real peace for your soul." From this remark alone we see that, with all the immense throng of "followers," she still remained wed to him by *interior knowledge*.[33]

In the final days of his life, Tolstoy literally fled from Sonya, heading first to a monastery to see the prior and then to a convent to see his sister. Eventually he died at the stationmaster's house at a railway station. As he lay dying both Sonya and a priest begged to see him, but Tolstoy's entourage refused, perhaps feeling that the shock of seeing the priest would be too much for a dying man. "With what we have said, it is ironical and symbolic that the Church and the wife should have been the ones forcibly kept away from the dying man."[34] One is reminded here of Lord Marchmain who in his last moment returned to the church despite the desperate efforts of some around him to keep him from it. It seems from his flight to the monastery and convent that Tolstoy too longed to find peace in the faith of his childhood.

This is a vivid example of the necessity of staying connected to the true feminine. And part of that feminine is the wisdom to receive not only the truth from above but the love and care that comes from the Father in heaven and from those around us who have His Holy Spirit. Thus we see that both men and women need to listen to that still, small voice. If we separate from the true feminine we can never be truly ourselves as God intended us to be.

A new heart I will give you, and a new spirit I will put within you; and I will take out of your flesh the heart of stone and give you a heart of flesh. And I will put my spirit within you, and cause you to walk in my statutes and be careful to observe my ordinances.

Ezekiel 36:26–27

Trust in the LORD with all your heart,
   and do not rely on your own insight.

Proverbs 3:5

Heavenly Father,

First I pray that You would enable me to trust You more completely. Please dissolve any barrier to trusting my Father in heaven that may exist. Help me to see You as You truly are and to know that I am Your beloved child. Prepare my soul to receive good things from You.

Give me ears to hear Your call to come to You, to find my home in You, to follow You first.

Next I ask that You would give me the wisdom that comes from above as a gift. I know that You rejoice to give good things to Your children, and I open my hands and my heart now to receive it.

Lord, with this gift I pray that I would have the eyes of my heart opened to see the world from Your perspective, with Your eyes.

Give me a vision of Your beauty that I might see You as You truly are.

Give me Your vision for my life.

Give me Your vision for the world.

Lord, You know the places within me that are not healthy and alive. Please send Your Holy Spirit to shed a light on those places that need strengthening or even res-

urrection. Bring about a beautiful integration of head and heart, and give me the health of Your Son.

It may be difficult for me to be truly feminine. Lord, please heal my fears of vulnerability and trust and deep feelings. Help me first to trust in You and then to see that Your perfect love does indeed cast out my fears. Please bless my intuition into hearts and insight into divine truth; please increase my capacity to love so that I may be a blessing to others. Help me to see that to be truly feminine is not to be passive and weak but glowing with life. I pray that I would come to a place of rest in who You have made me to be and that I would have a greater capacity to BE in Your presence than ever before.

It may be difficult for me to receive the true masculine. Lord, please heal my fear of responsibility and decision-making. Help me to know that You are my refuge and strength, that You are my rock. May I reflect You in my capacity to create good and lasting things. Please strengthen my will and give me new courage and insight in the face of adversity. I pray that I would imitate Your Son as I seek to combine strength with gentleness and to treat others as He treated them. I ask that You would enable me to protect and care for those I love but not fear being protected and cared for.

Help me to listen to You and not to the world in receiving my call to the work You have for me to do in this lifetime.

Please give me a new respect for both men and women so that I may always seek to encourage and not tear down.

Thank You that all of this is possible because Your Son died for my sin. Thank You for the wonderful destiny You have planned for all of Your children.
I pray these things in the name of Jesus,
Amen.

5

The Ennobler

"I was wishing that I came of a more honourable lineage."
"You come of the Lord Adam and the Lady Eve," said
Aslan. "And that is both honour enough to erect the head
of the poorest beggar, and shame enough to bow the
shoulders of the greatest emperor on earth. Be content."
Caspian bowed.

C. S. Lewis[1]

To ennoble means "to elevate in degree, excellence, or
respect; dignify; exalt."[2] By placing such value on
another, by calling forth the true self, we are imitating
God in His love for us. Only God can give us our true
selves, our true identity, purpose, and calling. But we
can help each other by recognizing all that is true and
good in another and encouraging it to live and to grow.
A woman can sometimes help a man to become the hero
that lies within, not by setting out to change his character or by expressing disappointment in him but by
loving him and keeping her eyes fixed on that potential
for greatness that lies within every human soul. By
"greatness" and "hero" we do not mean remarkable
deeds of physical strength or fame and fortune. Rather,
acts of courage, self-sacrifice, and dedication to doing
what is right make the true man of God—the sort of man

we see in Joseph with Mary, and always imitating Jesus in His true masculinity. When we are striving to be all that God intends for us to be then we are heroes and heroines.

Leanne Payne speaks of calling forth the true self and also of "magnanimity." The dictionary definition of this word is "the quality of being high-minded, noble, or *great-souled*."[3] God puts dreams and visions in our hearts; He gives us hope. He does not call us to diminish these dreams or to kill that hope but to put into action His vision for our lives.

> We as makers do not create in this way, out of nothing. Strictly speaking, only He can ever be called a Creator. But we, in His image, "make" according to the creative principle. . . . An idea or a thought "comes" to us; then we see with our mind's eye (i.e. we imagine) the painting, the building, the book, the project—whether the work of a conference, the creative work of parenting, or prayer for healing, etc. We see it, if ever so vaguely, as the finished whole. Then as *makers*, we work hard to uncover the work that now has form (if only in the imagination) and therefore an existence apart from ourselves. If we are Christians, there is an added dimension, for we know that we are collaborating with the Spirit of our Creator God to bring to light this work of art.[4]

This calling is a "great" and magnanimous one, and we cannot obey it in isolation. We have seen that men and women need each other in order to become all that God intends for them to be. In the case of Tolstoy and his wife, Sonya, she intuited the real and used all of her giftedness to call forth the best in her husband. This would be a situation where a true attempt is made to ennoble another.

We shall see further and more successful examples of this in *A Tale of Two Cities* and *The Secret Garden*, for the success of such an attempt depends on both man and woman working in harmony. Here we reflect God in seeing the potential in a fellow creature. However, there are other circumstances where a woman has not been able to receive either her or man's true giftedness, and her vision of their relationship and what she has to give him becomes distorted. The result of this may be at the very least a crushing of her true self; at worst, when the man with whom she is in relationship is unhealthy and the false feminine meets the false masculine, this attempt can be truly destructive. An example of a meeting such as this may be found in *Can You Forgive Her?* Here we see the difference between ennobling and disappearing into someone else's life.

A decision to live for someone else always has disastrous results. The heroine of this book is extremely gifted but tries to live through a man, hoping to inspire him to reach his full potential. To do this, the false feminine in her is attracted to the false masculine in one of the male characters; he is cold, distant, aggressive, and selfish. The man involved has other goals in mind, and the woman systematically puts to death her true self while addressing the false self in the man she thinks she loves, thereby doing them no good and potential harm. Only God's Spirit can instruct us how to discern between the true and the false self in ourselves and others. As we become healthier, not only will our discernment be sharper, but we will inevitably be attracted to spiritual and emotional health in other people.

In addressing the dangers of being an ennobler, it is important to point out the opposite of ennoblement—when men and women are in competition with each other. This is where stereotypes must be cast aside and the real distinction made between true and false feminine, true and false masculine. For the false feminine is not only passivity but manipulation; the false masculine is not only aggression but coldness. Examples of women who are truly feminine but have embraced the true masculine have already been mentioned: Madame Curie, Joan of Arc, Teresa of Avila.

The woman in competition with her husband has not accepted that she is *other* from man. The generosity of spirit that is the opposite of envy is lost and with it a part of the true feminine. At the same time that drivenness, the competition taken almost to the level of a desire to destroy, is not the true masculine drive to make and to create but is the false masculine.

A gift or strength under the sovereignty of God is a beautiful thing; it becomes its true self. But in a sinful world it is important to be aware that something beautiful can be twisted out of recognition. The special giftedness that allows a woman to see into the hearts of those she loves and call forth what is truly there has the potential for feeding the false self of both parties if she does not recognize that she is *other* and free to give generously. However, in the hands of God it can be part of a wonderful collaboration of hearts and minds, the masculine and the feminine meeting and delighting in one another as they were intended to do.

Mary in The Secret Garden
Frances Hodgson Burnett

Magic as White as Snow

When Mary found this garden it looked quite dead. . . . Then something began pushing things up out of the soil and making things out of nothing. One day things weren't there and another they were. . . . I keep saying to myself, "What is it? What is it?" It's something. It can't be nothing! I don't know its name so I call it Magic. . . . Magic is always pushing and drawing and making things out of nothing. Everything is made out of Magic, leaves and trees, flowers and birds, badgers and foxes and squirrels and people. So it must be all around us. In this garden—in all the places. The Magic in this garden has made me stand up and I know I am going to live to be a man.

Frances Hodgson Burnett[5]

If there is one book among those covered here that could suffer from the effects of overanalysis, it is Frances Hodgson Burnett's (1849–1924) story, *The Secret Garden*. There are two reasons for this. First, the primary message of bringing new life to that which was dead is so clear and unmistakable that we are then left with the task of attempting to psychoanalyze the children in the story, not to mention their parents. While some basic observations along these lines are important, such an attempt is not the purpose of this book. On the contrary, one of the primary roads to healing for two children and one adult in *The Secret Garden* is that they learn to look outside themselves and find, with some relief, that the world does not revolve around them.

Nor is it likely that Frances Hodgson Burnett hoped her readers would spend a great deal of time considering the pre-garden and post-garden emotions of Mary Lennox and her cousin Colin Craven. As each child becomes healthy it is as if they were never ill; the point is not that the process of healing is so easy but that it can be so *complete*. For those who have suffered and received healing, it can be difficult to accept that happiness does not have to be tinged with hopelessness and that one never has to be isolated and friendless again. It is difficult to accept the responsibility that happiness brings; ennoblement can be frightening. It is one thing to be the young plant slowly growing with proper nourishment and tender care into a tree: it is another to be that grown tree firmly rooted in the ground and planted by streams of living water, as strong as the cedars of Lebanon. There are also those who long for healing but believe that there are some things that they simply must live with, that God cannot do. But these children reach for help with both hands and have no trouble accepting it and living out of their true self once discovered.

Each of these children starts off as lonely, self-absorbed, and afraid. But once the process of ennoblement is well under way, they find it difficult to recall their former selves except by turning the pages backward. The children themselves come to look upon their old selves as a source of amusement. They come to expect good things from life, and at the same time even

Dickon, who has lived on the moors all his life, is filled with wonder at the approach of spring. The adult rereading *The Secret Garden* can treasure this glimpse of wholeness for what it is and try to imitate some of the simple steps taken to encourage that health in themselves and those they love.

Second, it is tempting to attempt to find a perfect balance between our own religious convictions, what we know about the beliefs of the author, and the spiritual dimensions of the book itself. The author, who clearly glimpsed Christian truth, was also acquainted with a variety of philosophies including Spiritualism, Theosophy, and Christian Science. She comes very close but seems to stop short of fully endorsing Christianity, at least in this particular work and in the words of Dickon's mother, Susan Sowerby. When, towards the end of the book the children are in the garden, Colin cries: "I feel— I feel as if I want to shout out something—something thankful, joyful!"[6], the old gardener Ben Weatherstaff suggests singing the doxology.

> Dickon stood out among the trees and rose-bushes and began to sing in quite a simple matter-of-fact way and in a nice strong boy voice:
>
> > *"Praise God from whom all blessings flow,*
> > *Praise Him all creatures here below,*
> > *Praise Him above ye Heavenly Host,*
> > *Praise Father, Son, and Holy Ghost.*
> > *Amen."*[7]

Dickon's mother comes into the garden while they are singing, and they explain the "Magic" to her.

> "Do you believe in Magic?" asked Colin. . . . "I do hope you do."

"That I do, lad," she answered. "I never knowed it by that name but what does th' name matter? I warrant they call it a different name i' France an' a different one i' Germany. Th' same thing as set th' seeds swellin' an' th' sun shinin' made thee a well lad an' it's th' Good Thing. . . . Never thee stop believin' in th' Big Good Thing an' knowin' th' world's full of it—an' call it what tha' likes. Tha' wert singin' to it when I come into th' garden. . . . The Magic listened when tha' sung th' Doxology. It would ha' listened to anything tha'd sung. It was th' joy that mattered. Eh! lad, lad—what's names to th' Joy Maker," and she gave his shoulders a quick soft pat again.[8]

The character of Susan Sowerby is quite prominent in the book, even when she is not physically present. However, in the various movie and stage productions of the novel she has a very small role and sometimes does not appear at all; certainly the singing of the doxology and all references to hymns and church are completely eliminated. Consequently, the "Magic" in several of these productions takes on a pagan quality that is the only false note in otherwise faithful renditions of the story. The earliest and most authentic (in tone if not in dialogue) movie version of *The Secret Garden* emphasizes the beauty of the garden and the relationships between the children as working the Magic, and there is no specific spiritual reference. If one is not going to mention Susan Sowerby or the singing of the doxology at this crucial moment in the book when the children feel they simply must thank *someone* for what has happened to them, it is probably best not to create a spiritual ritual to replace these things. Although Susan's comment about "th' Big Good Thing" is not Christian, at least she is in the book.

Whatever the beliefs and intentions of the author, which will not be dealt with in detail here, the importance and beauty of the creation is central to this book—that something is made out of nothing by Someone. While man is the pinnacle of God's creation, God spent the first five days creating the rest of the world and "saw that it was good" (Genesis 1). If the creation is good in God's estimation, then surely it must be so in ours, and we must treat it in keeping with its true worth, as having come from the mouth of God. In *The Secret Garden* we see Mary relating to the creation as in a vibrant relationship; the fresh air of the moors and the mystery of the garden begin to draw her out of herself, and her first friend is a robin.

She treats the variety of flowers as if they have distinct personalities and can respond to her. This atmosphere is reminiscent of three great Christian souls: Saint Francis of Assisi, C. S. Lewis, and J. R. R. Tolkien.

Burnett, Tolkien, and Lewis all had the gift of seeing the creation as the treasure that it really is, even investing certain aspects of it with human qualities. Symbolically, they echo the intent of God when He entrusted His creation to the dominion and care of man. Man thus has the capacity to ennoble the creation—or to harm it. Francis of Assisi knew that God had made everything with the capacity to bring glory to Him and had a remarkable love for all living things because they had come from the heart of God.

We know from the words of Jesus that God Himself has ennobled His creation, bestowing a beauty upon it that we often take for granted and causing it to reflect His loving care.

> Consider the lilies of the field, how they grow; they neither toil nor spin; yet I tell you, even Solomon in all his glory was not arrayed like one of these. But if God so

clothes the grass of the field, which today is alive and tomorrow is thrown into the oven, will He not much more clothe you, O men of little faith?

Matthew 6:28–30

Like the lilies of the field (and it is interesting that Colin's dead mother, who loved gardens and created the secret garden, was called Lilias), the story of Mary and Colin's ennoblement—that process by which they become fully alive and hope-filled human beings—is remarkable in its simplicity. There is a simple recognition of need on both their parts that is quite touching. This is clear from the readiness and thirst with which they respond to good things, like baby birds crying out for food while still in the nest and eagerly consuming whatever their mother brings them. Ironically, shortly after Mary's discovery of the garden, Dickon likens her to a thrush tending her nest. She has become the "mother" and will soon be ready to help her cousin Colin. Indeed, his need becomes the next stage in her ennoblement; in addition to the garden, she now has someone other than herself to care for.

There are three simple keys to Mary's ennoblement, and this is one of them: *She is given the opportunity to care about something and someone outside of herself, and she takes that opportunity.* She learns about an enclosed garden with a door no one can find and a key buried by her uncle ten years before. "This gave her so much to think of that she began to be quite interested and feel that she was not sorry that she had come to Misselthwaite Manor. In India she had always felt too hot and too languid to care much about anything. The fact was that the fresh wind from the moor had begun to blow the cobwebs out of her young brain and to waken her up a little."[9] Mary makes it her goal to get inside that garden, and she succeeds. Once inside, her energy and thoughts are completely consumed with bringing it to life again. She hears someone crying in the middle of the night and wanders the halls of the vast house until she finds her cousin Colin, who has spent his life in bed and is convinced he is going to die. "I never had a secret," he said, "except that one about not living to grow up. They don't know I know that so it is a sort of secret."[10] Mary takes an immediate interest in Colin, and soon her time is divided between him and the garden. She moves from a life empty of friendship and interests to having many people who like her and whom she likes. And now she has two goals to work towards: to bring the garden to life, and to bring Colin into the garden. As she works towards these goals she blooms into life herself.

One of the most important things Mary does to show true love for her cousin and to encourage his ennoblement is to confront his conviction about his illness and early death and the fear underlying this conviction. She does so using a means that no one has used with Colin before—she contradicts him and accuses him of selfishness. She also deals in facts instead of encouraging the fear he has known all his life. Colin had been surrounded by adults who, out of ignorance of his true condition, spoke with assurance of his supposed deformity and inevitable death at an early age.

> "There's not a single lump there!" she said at last. "There's not a lump as big as a pin—except backbone lumps, and you can only feel them because you're thin. . . . There's not a lump as big as a pin! If you ever say there is again, I shall laugh!"
>
> No one but Colin himself knew what effect those crossly spoken childish words had on him. If he had ever had any one to talk to about his secret terrors—if he had ever dared to let himself ask questions—if he had had

childish companions and had not lain on his back in the huge closed house, breathing an atmosphere heavy with the fears of people who were most of them ignorant and tired of him, he would have found out that most of his fright and illness was created by himself. But he had lain and thought of himself and his aches and weariness for hours and days and months and years. And now that an angry unsympathetic little girl insisted obstinately that he was not as ill as he thought he was he actually felt as if she might be speaking the truth. . . .

"Do you think—I could—live to grow up?" he said.[11]

While Mary rightly accuses Colin of the self-absorption for which he must take responsibility, she is also angry at the fear and deception that have hurt her cousin and is the first one to point out that, quite simply, there is nothing physically wrong with him; it is all a lie. By pointing out the truth to him she is confirming her own freedom from the misery and self-absorption that had held her captive. Shortly after this she shares the secret of the garden with him, and before long a natural process of restoration begins when he is surrounded by fresh air, sun, animals, trees and flowers, and the companionship of other children.

This brings us to the next key to the life of the garden in Mary's heart: *the importance of simple, practical things to bring about good health, and how much the physical, emotional, mental, and spiritual aspects of our being are intertwined.* Both Mary and Colin were neglected by their parents. Mary's parents ignored her and entrusted her to the care of a servant who did not like her. Colin's father's desire for his own death may have been projected onto his son; at any rate he certainly took no care for his well-being on any level. Moreover, these children grew up with limited physical or mental exercise, and both grew into bored, listless, physically weak ten-year-olds. Lack of exercise led to decreased appetite, disturbed sleep, and a certain frailty. The heat in India and the stagnant air of Colin's bedroom contributed to this result. Over time, the world and its charms became less and less interesting, and Mary and Colin became the center of their own lives, defending themselves against loneliness and neglect and assuming a self-importance that was catered to by servants who had to put up with them.

From the first, the simple act of running on the wintry grounds of the Yorkshire estate (and eating because of the appetite generated by the running) is the beginning of greater physical well-being for Mary. It turns out that gardens and fresh air are good for Colin too. A similar transformation takes place in him until "as an imitation of a boy who was a confirmed invalid he was a disgraceful sight."[12] And, becoming physically stronger through good food, exercise, and natural, unbroken sleep, their emotional fragility is healed as well. In *The Secret Garden* there is a direct connection between physical and emotional well-being. This is of course not always the case, but the story of Mary and Colin does reflect a simple truth that is sometimes overlooked.

The final key to the children's transformation is that *taking in the good pushes out the bad*. This is to be distinguished from focusing on the bad for the purpose of removing it. Mary and Colin's energies are not directed at removing their selfishness, loneliness, and fear. Instead, the focus is on good things: bringing the garden to life, relationships with people like Martha, Dickon, and Susan Sowerby; spring, animals, laughing together.

So long as Colin shut himself up in his room and thought only of his fears and weakness and his detestation of people who looked at him and reflected hourly on lumps and early death, he was a hysterical, half-crazy little hypochondriac who knew nothing of the sunshine and the spring and also did not know that he could get well and could stand upon his feet if he tried to do it. When new beautiful thoughts began to push out the old hideous ones, life began to come back to him, his blood ran healthily through his veins and strength poured into him like a flood. His scientific experiment was quite practical and simple and there was nothing weird about it at all. Much more surprising things can happen to any one who, when a disagreeable or discouraged thought comes into his mind, just has the sense to remember in time and push it out by putting in an agreeably determinedly courageous one. Two things cannot be in one place.

> *"Where you tend a rose, my lad,*
> *A thistle cannot grow."*[13]

As their lives fill with new interests and hopes, the sadness of their former lives is naturally pushed out for lack of room. This reflects a powerful Christian truth about good and evil. As Christ takes up residence in the heart all sorts of things that are incompatible with His Holy Spirit are pushed out. Thus, one should not be surprised at the things that come unexpectedly to a conscious level that were previously buried and quite content to rest undisturbed in the hidden regions of the heart. When one focuses on God in prayer His power has the capacity to send the evil one fleeing.

Both the garden and the children are neglected for ten years, but that neglect could not destroy them. They are both "wick" as Dickon describes the roses in the garden—seemingly dead on the outside but alive on the inside, just waiting for some care. Moreover, there is a "domino effect" with ennoblement, for we all need each other. One might say that Mary is ennobled by the garden and by Dickon, Martha, the Robin, Ben, Susan Sowerby—all those who take an interest in her and see that she is "wick"—and that Colin is ennobled in the same way but this time with Mary leading the way, and that Colin then ennobles his father, who appears in the garden in the final pages of the book, seeking the son he has neglected all his life. Not only are the children healthier and happier; they have hope for the future. For this too is a feature of ennoblement: the engendering of a vision that is bigger than oneself and a hope that it will come to pass. Colin expresses it best:

> "I'm well! I'm well!" said Colin again, and his face went quite red all over.
>
> He had known it before in a way, he had hoped it and felt it and thought about it, but just at that minute something had rushed all through him—a sort of rapturous belief and realization and it had been so strong that he could not help calling out.
>
> "I shall live forever and ever and ever!" he cried grandly. "I shall find out thousands and thousands of things. I shall find out about people and creatures and everything that grows—like Dickon—and I shall never stop making Magic. I'm well! I'm well!"[14]

Alice in *Can You Forgive Her?*
Anthony Trollope

The Dangers of Seeking Ennoblement in the Wrong Place

Upon the whole it was a grievous task to her in these days,—this having to do something with her life. Was it not all vain and futile? As for that girl's dream of the joys of love which she had once dreamed,—that had gone from her slumbers, never to return. How might she best make herself useful,—useful in some sort that might gratify her ambition;—that was now the question which seemed to her to be of most importance.

Anthony Trollope[15]

It is a wonderful thing to walk with someone in the process of ennoblement—pointing out the good and true in another and encouraging the growth of these things, affirming the gifts that God has given another, helping someone to come into their true identity as a child of God. Encouragement, exhortation, wisdom, and humility are needed for this noble task of pointing the way to the truly abundant life offered by God in Jesus. We are all called to do this. In *The Secret Garden* the children are focused on enjoying the creation and helping one another. However, there is a crucial difference between

168

this and hoping to acquire both identity and purpose or to be ennobled through a relationship with another human being—or believing that one can give these things to another if we love them enough. This is impossible since all of these things come as gifts from God alone.

In Anthony Trollope's (1815–1882) 1864 novel *Can You Forgive Her?* we have the case of a woman, Alice Vavasor, who wants to give her life purpose and thinks that this can best be accomplished through the ambitions of her husband. She also hopes to "do him good . . . to save him from ruin, and help him to honour and fortune."[16] Indeed, she is encouraged to see herself as his ennobler by his sister who tells Alice that "the only thing wanting to make him thoroughly good, is a wife"[17] and that Alice should only marry someone if she can "marry him with that sort of worshipping, idolatrous love which makes a girl proud as well as happy in her marriage."[18] Like all of Trollope's most prominent characters, especially in the six Palliser Novels, and in keeping with his own preoccupation, she believes a political career to be the highest achievement imaginable: "Let me have the honour and glory of marrying a man who has gained a seat in the Parliament of Great Britain! Of all positions which a man may attain that, to me, is the grandest."[19] Alice becomes engaged to her cousin, George Vavasor, an aggressive, calculating, and violent man whose primary motivations in wishing to marry Alice are obtaining her money and triumphing over his rival, John Grey.

Alice's motivation in becoming engaged to George is also twofold: a vague desire for a purpose in life beyond her marriage, and false guilt that builds to a truly destructive self-hatred. Indeed, the title of this first volume of the Palliser Novels should be not *Can You Forgive Her?* but *Can She Forgive Herself?* Alice experiences guilt when she ends her engagement to John Grey; the guilt is so extreme that she decides to marry her cousin George because she is convinced that true love is over for her and that she might as well devote her life to a worthy cause from which both she and George may benefit. Her ambition and her guilt are enmeshed with one another as her "jilting" of John affects her sensitive conscience greatly. Feeling guilt after causing pain to a loved one is legitimate, but Alice's self-reproach is so severe that it propels her into a foolish decision to reject love in favor of what can only be called a marriage of convenience.

Trollope rightly says that in agreeing to marry her cousin George without love Alice "sinned against the softness of her feminine nature."[20] Nonetheless, the reader can readily forgive Alice, and the author himself tells us that he has forgiven her despite his emphasis on her sin, which is extreme even for the time.

Alice is intelligent, complicated, and a model of integrity; unfortunately, when confronted with her own failings she does the worst thing she can possibly do. Despite the fact that she repents her decision and realizes that she still loves John, and instead of accepting John's forgiveness, which is so immediate that it is hardly a matter for discussion from his point of view, she holds on to her guilt and attaches herself to George, who will inevitably cause her the pain she feels she deserves.

Alice's guilt becomes false and is hardly distinguishable from pride when she cannot receive the forgiveness that is offered to her; she exaggerates her fault out of all proportion to reality and takes a self-destructive action. Her desire to be ennobled by a great purpose becomes false only when it is either vague and abstract or inseparable from politics. Viewing her life as something of great value is right and healthy, but she becomes confused in thinking that in marrying John she would be losing her true self while a life with George would

170

answer the question that reverberates through every soul: Who am I?

> With all her doubts Alice never doubted her love for Mr. Grey. Nor did she doubt his character, nor his temper, nor his means. But she had gone on thinking of the matter till her mind had become filled with some undefined idea of the importance to her of her own life. . . .
> A woman's life is important to her,—as is that of a man to him,—not chiefly in regard to that which she should do with it. The chief thing for her to look to is the manner in which that something shall be done. . . .
> Alice Vavasor was ever asking herself that question, and had by degrees filled herself with a vague idea that there was a something to be done; a something over and beyond, or perhaps altogether beside that marrying and having two children;—if only she knew what it was. She had filled herself, or had been filled by her cousins, with an undefined ambition that made her restless without giving her any real food for her mind.[21]

In the course of the novel, both John and George show their true colors. George's character transformation is somewhat predictable. At first we believe him to be wild and easily angered but talented and charismatic as well. Later we see him consumed by rage and pride, even attempting to murder John Grey and subsequently leaving the country. John, however, is revealed as one of the most appealing characters in all the Trollope novels. Alice's rejection of him is based on her conviction that his life in Cambridgeshire would be too dull and quiet for one such as herself, longing for a political life in London. Moreover, she is disappointed at his lack of ambition and sees him as unexciting (George compares John to milk and himself to brandy). At first, it is difficult for the reader not to be somewhat convinced of this as well and to agree with Alice's father that John is a little too sure of himself. As the story unfolds, however, we see his inner being come to light—his courage as he protects Alice from George; his compassion towards Alice in her plight; his remarkable level of insight into her character that shows a depth Alice never guessed at; his perseverance and humility as he attempts to win Alice back.

It is also lovely to watch as John admits to being wrong in his lack of interest in the world around him, and against all odds he decides in favor of the political career Alice has always longed for. In the end "he left her no alternative but to be happy. But there still clung to her what I fear we must call a perverseness of obstinacy, a desire to maintain the resolution she had made,—a wish that she might be allowed to undergo the punishment she had deserved. She was as a prisoner who would fain cling to his prison after pardon has reached him, because he is conscious that the pardon is undeserved."[22] This remark reveals Alice's tendency to "make a virtue of misery," and it takes the efforts of many fellow characters to bring out the best in her and her true desire for well-being and a healthy marriage.

When love and respect are placed before a personal agenda of need, Alice and John can participate in the process of ennoblement. Forgiveness is given and received. Through Alice, John begins to see that he has more to give to life than he had been willing to give while living quietly in Cambridgeshire; Alice thus realizes her ambition, but first she must discard the notion of marrying without love or that she is not worthy to marry with it. This ending works, for Alice was not wrong in doubting her ability to be content with a certain type of lifestyle. She will unquestionably make a good politician's wife. Indeed, at a later period in history, with her intelligence, integrity, sensitive conscience, stubbornness, passion, and refusal to compromise she would have made an excellent politician herself.

Lucie in *A Tale of Two Cities*
Charles Dickens

Inspiring a Sacrificial Love

I am sure that he is capable of good things, gentle things, even magnanimous things.

Charles Dickens[23]

In Charles Dickens's *A Tale of Two Cities* (1859) cynical and dissolute English lawyer Sydney Carton chooses to die by the guillotine so that someone else may live. However, this is not so much a story of transformation as of resurrection, the rising to life of that which was dead or buried. Carton does not hope to improve upon the raw material of his sadly wasted life; rather, his encounter with Lucie Manette (the woman destined to be the wife of his client Charles Darnay who has been wrongly accused of treason) inspires a truly selfless love that leads to a destiny greater than any he had previously imagined for himself. It is not his old man made better but a secret life coming out of hiding and growing into a new thing altogether, like a smoldering ember buried under piles of ashes that is uncovered and blown into life by Lucie.

173

A fire soon burns where a cold black hearth had been; by the end the fire has become a beacon. Not long after his meeting with Lucie, Carton is behaving in ways that are uncharacteristic, such as sharing his deepest regrets and hopes with Lucie and asking the forgiveness of Charles Darnay, his rival for her love ("He was not improved in habits, or in looks, or in manner; but there was a certain rugged air of fidelity about him, which was new to the observation of Charles Darnay"[24]); by the end his actions are radical, sacrificial, faith-filled.

One thing is certain: Carton's secret life becomes less of a secret from the moment he sees Lucie. And yet what is it about her that ennobles so beautifully? Perhaps more than any heroine we have encountered, except for Kitty of *Anna Karenin*, Lucie shows that there are those who ennoble simply by existing rightly; her presence, voice, movement, and especially the "sweet compassion" that Carton refers to several times in the novel all provide a calm, meaningful place, a projection of the intangible, transcendent feminine. She is described as "ever busily winding the golden thread that bound them all together, weaving the service of her happy influence through the tissue of all their lives, and making it predominate nowhere."[25]

When I first mentioned including Dickens in this book about heroines of literature to a friend, her comment was, "*Are* there any strong women in Dickens?" I was not surprised by this question; there are many female characters in Dickens's novels who are presented as helpless victims of some form of abuse or who appear to lack depth and complexity. However, the more I read of Dickens the more I see that, despite the ambivalence toward women that is sometimes expressed in the treatment of his female characters, he vividly portrays certain feminine virtues with great accuracy. Hence, for example, the courage and perception of a Betsey Trotwood or the capacity to ennoble of a Lucie Manette. Nowhere is Dickens's respect for women and awareness of the influence they can have for good on those around them more apparent than in *A Tale of Two Cities*. All of the virtues discussed here are present in Lucie, and all are held together by a faith that is implicit in her actions and often explicit in her words. Lucie ennobles with beauty, compassion, and love.

There are frequent references to Lucie's beauty, and this deserves some consideration: "His eyes rested on a short, slight, pretty figure, a quantity of golden hair, a pair of blue eyes that met his own with an inquiring look, and a forehead with a singular capacity (remembering how young and smooth it was), of lifting and knitting itself into an expression that was not quite one of perplexity, or wonder, or alarm, or merely of a bright fixed attention, though it included all the four expressions."[26]

Christians are rightly taught to place little or no importance on physical appearance but to look instead for inner beauty. However, the two are sometimes inseparable, as in the case of Lucie. Moreover, beauty takes many forms and we are all drawn to it, whether it is the beauty of a sunrise, a garden in the spring, a symphony by Beethoven, or a man or a woman. This is because physical beauty, even of a human being destined to age and die, is an echo of the promise and the permanence of eternal life. Even if it is not our lot to be as beautiful as Lucie Manette in this life, it is important for us to know that such things are possible, that potential for beauty is what matters and that it will one day be realized throughout creation. Literature allows us to enjoy the physical beauty of a character and to give it the same worth as the beauty of anything that has come from the mind of God. Moreover, Lucie's beauty is an extension of the radiance in her heart and soul, and we can hope for such a transformation to illuminate our faces.

Lucie's compassion for those who are weak or in distress is tested throughout the book, in her relationships with both father and husband, and with Sydney Carton. Lucie is fully aware of Sydney's character, but she does not judge him. Instead, Lucie seems to see straight through to that smoldering ember within Sydney and offers that hope as a gift with every word she speaks to him.

"I am like one who died young. All my life might have been."

"No, Mr. Carton. I am sure the best part of it might still be; I am sure you might be much, much worthier of yourself." . . .

"Since I knew you, I have been troubled by a remorse that I thought would never reproach me again, and have heard whispers from old voices impelling me upward, that I thought were silent for ever. I have had unformed ideas of striving afresh, beginning anew, shaking off sloth and sensuality, and fighting out the abandoned fight. A dream, all a dream, that ends in nothing, and leaves the sleeper where he lay down, but I wish you to know that you inspired it . . . know with what a sudden mastery you kindled me, heap of ashes that I am, into fire—a fire, however, inseparable in its nature from myself, quickening nothing, lighting nothing, doing no service, idly burning away." . . .

"Since the state of your mind that you describe is, at all events, attributable to some influence of mine—that is what I mean, if I can make it plain—can I use no influence to serve you? Have I no power for good, with you, at all?" . . .

"Let me carry through the rest of my misdirected life, the remembrance that I opened my heart to you, last of all the world; and that there was something left in me at this time which you could deplore and pity."

"Which I entreated you to believe, again and again, most fervently, with all my heart, was capable of better things, Mr. Carton!" . . .

"My last supplication of all, is this. . . . For you, and for any dear to you, I would do anything. If my career were of that better kind that there was any opportunity or capacity of sacrifice in it, I would embrace any sacrifice for you and for those dear to you . . . Oh Miss Manette, when the little picture of a happy father's face looks up in yours, when you see your own bright beauty springing up anew at your feet, think now and then that there is a man who would give his life, to keep a life you love beside you!"[27]

Lucie's love and compassion are returned to her a thousandfold when Sydney sees the opportunity for exchanging his life for that of her husband, who is wrongly accused of treason in revolutionary France, and of making good on his promise to give his life to keep a life she loves beside her. When Lucie is convinced that her husband will die, her faith is uppermost in her mind: "I can bear it, dear Charles. I am supported from above: don't suffer for me. . . . We shall not be separated long. I feel that this will break my heart by and by; but I will do my duty while I can."[28] And as Sydney Carton chooses to sacrifice out of the love inspired by her, her faith becomes his; the code phrase for reuniting Lucie with her father—"Recalled to Life"—could be used of Sydney's reuniting with his true self, so long buried.

The words of John's Gospel (see 11:25–26), repeated by Sydney once he has made the decision to give his life for one he loves, are the words that reunite him with the Savior he is unconsciously imitating: "I am the Resurrection and the Life, saith the Lord: he that believeth in me, though he were dead, yet shall he live: and whosoever liveth and believeth in me shall never die!" And, as

we have seen, there is always a domino effect to ennoblement. Sydney ultimately affects other lives as powerfully as Lucie has affected his. He begins as he waits
for death with a young woman also condemned to die
in the midst of the madness of the revolution; he speaks
to her with compassion and shares his own courage and
hope with her. Her response shows how she in her turn
has been ennobled by Carton: "But for you, dear stranger,
I should not be so composed, for I am naturally a poor
little thing, faint of heart; nor should I have been able to
raise my thoughts to Him who was put to death, that we
might have hope and comfort here to-day. I think you
were sent to me by Heaven."[29]

Human beings are capable of both great and terrible things. Although our inheritance as children of God is in heaven, we live in a fallen world, and we are surrounded by both good and evil every day. Paul speaks of the challenges of being ambassadors for Christ in enemy territory:

> For it is God who said, "Let light shine out of darkness," who has shone in our hearts to give the light of the knowledge of the glory of God in the face of Christ. But we have this treasure in earthen vessels, to show that the transcendent power belongs to God and not to us. . . . So we do not lose heart. Though our outer nature is wasting away, our inner nature is being renewed every day. For this slight momentary affliction is preparing for us an eternal weight of glory beyond all comparison.
>
> 2 Corinthians 4:6–7, 16–17

Although the treasure is in earthen vessels, let us remember that it is a treasure; although the transcendent power belongs to God we have access to it; although the source of the light is God, this same light shines in our hearts; although we continue to suffer from our own sin and the effects of the sin of others, we are destined to bear "an eternal weight of glory beyond all comparison." Thus we see that, only as ennobled by the new life in Christ, we are as capable of magnanimous things as Sydney Carton.

We receive our ennoblement as a gift from the only One who can work such a change in the human soul. When Jesus takes up residence in our hearts we are ennobled by "him who by the power at work within us is able to do far more abundantly than all that we ask or think" (Eph. 3:20). The power at work within us is His Holy Spirit. God is the Source of all good things, the Living Water, the Vine. We are the branches, His body, His temple, His ambassadors. When we have the privilege to participate in the ennoblement of a fellow creature, we are collaborating with God as He gives us eyes to see with His love, compassion, hope, and vision: "We are God's fellow workers," but "no other foundation can any one lay than that which is laid, which is Jesus Christ" (1 Cor. 3:9, 11). Jesus said, "Apart from me you can do nothing" (John 15:5). Any lasting ennoblement must start with the new life to be found in Him, where we identify with Him in both His crucifixion and resurrection. Our old sinful self, separated from the lover of our souls, is dead and buried; the new self rises to life in the Spirit.

When we help another to become all that God intends them to be, we must point the way to the truth and give no attention to what is false. There is a new creation that needs nourishment. Mary Lennox is a perfect example of this in her absolute refusal to engage in a dialogue with Colin about something she knew to be a lie. Rather than commiserating with him, and thus fueling the lie, the fear, and the hopelessness that gripped her cousin, she boldly stated that there was no truth in his belief that he would become deformed and die young. She even took the risk by becoming angry with him for his self-absorption and not taking him as seriously as he took himself. Instead, she insisted on introducing him to the *reality* of the garden in spring and of Dickon and his animals, and encouraged him in his hope that he would not only get well but would one day do great things as a scientist to help others. At the same time, she knew how much he had suffered and was kind and gentle with him, separating that which genuinely deserved sympathy from that which deserved to be ignored. In this way she helped to call forth Colin's true self, which had been asleep for so many years.

Many people live for years with pain they never thought could fade from memory like a dream and underneath that pain, dreams they never thought could become reality. When one begins to realize that one has "settled" or has identified himself or herself with mediocrity, the barriers that have thus far halted ennoblement can loom even larger at first. These obstacles are often quite formidable—hopelessness that may have taken up residence in the heart through a series of painful events, false messages from others that have been received as truth, even laziness. There are times when there is no vision for the future there at all; in other cases there is a vision but also a litany of excuses beginning with "I could never do that or be that because . . ." The process of ennoblement must begin with asking the Father in heaven for everything that is needed, whether it be healing, the gift of hope, or His unique vision for our lives. But as God's "fellow workers" we can help our brothers and sisters by encouraging everything in them that is good and true, by naming a lie when we see it and replacing that with the truth, by refusing to entertain what is false and unreal, by tenderly caring for those who are suffering and pointing them to the cross of Christ. Ennoblement may be regarded as part of the sanctification process that is the work of God's Spirit within us. Thus, we must accept the fact that it is the destiny of every Christian to one day be like Jesus Christ.

Beloved, we are God's children now; it does not yet appear what we shall be, but we know that when he appears we shall be like him, for we shall see him as he is. And every one who thus hopes in him purifies himself as he is pure.

1 John 3:2–3

Prayer

We were buried therefore with him by baptism into death, so that as Christ was raised from the dead by the glory of the Father, we too might walk in newness of life.

Romans 6:4

Dear Jesus,

I ask that You would remind me every day that I am a new creation, indwelled by Your Holy Spirit. Please fill me anew with that Spirit.

Help me to take my stand with You in Your death and Your resurrection. Thank You for taking my sin on the cross, making it possible for me to become like You, "partaking of the divine nature." It is my longing to grow in that likeness each day. I pray that others would see You in me.

I pray that I would never look to anyone else but You for my identity and calling or to give me the "great" soul I long for. But give me the grace to receive the help of others who want me to grow.

Lord, You have made it possible for me to be a hero or a heroine, capable of noble and magnanimous acts, of great and good things, capable of living out any vision You have for my life—a vision from the heart of God. Thank

You that such things are real, that my faith is as full of wonder as a fairy tale, except that it is true. I pray that You would give me opportunities to bring glory to You, the lover of our souls, the ennobler of our souls.

Knowing that, help me to forget myself and to be an ennobler of others, helping them to become all that You have created them to be. Give me Your eyes of love that I might see how precious each soul is, and how individually gifted by You. I ask for both encouragement and exhortation. Give me the gift of discernment so that I can distinguish between the truth and a lie, and give me the courage to speak. Help me to never sacrifice truth in the name of love.

I ask these things in Your name,
Amen.

Epilogue

It is my hope that this book has communicated three things. First, that well-chosen works of fiction are more than just entertainment (although they are that as well); they can call us up and out of ourselves to our true potential as people indwelled by Christ. I believe that many people underestimate the impact of fiction on their minds and souls, both for good and ill. Any woman can be a storybook heroine; she can discover virtues in fictional characters who inspire her to new hopes and dreams, and she can learn from their mistakes. Second, that women are blessed with special strengths and gifts that need to be recognized and embraced, both for their own well-being and happiness, and to bless others and bring glory to God. It is vital to call attention to this in an age when the media and the arts tend to emphasize a false understanding of both men and women, crushing these true gifts and making virtue meaningless. Women today can benefit from a deeper understanding of their special giftedness and the meaning of femininity from a Christian perspective. Finally, I wanted to bring these two facts together and show how the hearts of women can be opened to new possibilities and be transformed through contact with good books.

It was not my intention to dissect the faith of the characters, either out of curiosity or as a measure against one's own faith, but rather to look at their words and actions and feelings and draw conclusions from them. Although the characters are grouped according to chapter, it is the virtue expressed by them that places them there, not an attempt to assign them a virtue. I felt that this would be a way of getting away from all stereotypes about femininity, both those found inside and outside the church, and taking a fresh look at what women can be, even in the imagination of a gifted writer. Nor was it my intention to present a spiritual biography of the authors concerned. While I have at times briefly commented on their faith, it would have been a disservice to these individuals to have attempted a presentation of their spiritual journeys in a book devoted to the characters they created. Each would be a book in itself. I certainly developed an even greater respect for these authors and the gift they gave the world through their writing. Finally, it was not my intention to imply that men do not possess the virtues discussed here in equal abundance with women; rather, I hoped to convey that women express these virtues in truly unique ways and have gifts to offer that are desperately needed.

A crucial point must be made in closing. As important as the acquisition of virtue is, we are not meant to pursue it as our primary goal. Christians are followers of Christ. Thus, our longing is not for what God can give us but for God Himself. In the words of Oswald Chambers, "Personal holiness is an effect, not a cause."[1] We can ask the Father, the Giver of all good gifts, for courage, wisdom, and the like and then determine to surround ourselves with all that He has provided to nourish our souls. If we focus on these things, including good books (or books touched with goodness), and most especially receiving the truth of His Word into our

souls and keeping our eyes on His Son, then we will
resemble Him more and more and, not as a goal but as
a result, know some of the virtues that find their source
in Him.

Both the children were looking up into the Lion's face
as he spoke these words. And all at once (they never
knew exactly how it happened) the face seemed to be a
sea of tossing gold in which they were floating, and such
a sweetness and power rolled about them and over them
and entered into them that they felt they had never really
been happy or wise or good, or even alive and awake,
before. And the memory of that moment stayed with
them always, so that as long as they both lived, if ever
they were sad or afraid or angry, the thought of all that
golden goodness, and the feeling that it was still there,
quite close, just around some corner or just behind some
door, would come back and make them sure, deep down
inside, that all was well.[2]

Notes

Preface

1. Edith Nesbit, *Harding's Luck* (1909; reprint, New York: Books of Wonder, 1998), 190–91.

2. I first encountered the terms "true feminine," "false feminine," "true masculine," and "false masculine" and a unique, groundbreaking discussion of these in the books of Leanne Payne.

3. A phrase used by C. S. Lewis in the seventh and last of The Chronicles of Narnia, *The Last Battle* (New York: Macmillan, 1956).

Part 1: The Lover

1. St. John of the Cross, *Dark Night of the Soul* (New York: Doubleday, 1990), 143.

2. Alice von Hildebrand, *Feminism and Femininity: A Catholic Perspective* (Irondale, Ala.: Eternal Word Television Network, 1997), television program.

3. C. S. Lewis, *The Voyage of the Dawn Treader* (New York: Macmillan, 1952), 131–32.

4. Leanne Payne, *Crisis in Masculinity* (Grand Rapids: Baker, A Hamewith Book, 1995), 87.

5. Henri Troyat, *Tolstoy* (New York: Doubleday, 1967), 305.

6. Ibid., 305–6.

7. Tolstoy, *War and Peace*, trans. with an introduction by Rosemary Edmonds (1869; reprint, Baltimore: Penguin, 1957), 1092.

8. von Hildebrand, *Feminism and Femininity*.

9. Sheldon Vanauken, *A Severe Mercy* (London: Hodder & Stoughton, 1977), 201.

10. Tolstoy, *War and Peace*, 494–95.

11. Ibid., 542–43.

12. Ibid., 1090–91.

13. Charlotte Brontë, *Jane Eyre* (1847; reprint, New York: Bantam, 1981), from the author's preface to the second edition.

14. Ibid., 127.

15. Ibid., 189.

16. Ibid., 205.

17. Ibid., 206.

18. Ibid., 301–2.

19. Ibid., 427–28.

20. Ibid., 30.

21. Ibid., 226–27.

22. C. S. Lewis, *Prince Caspian* (New York: Macmillan, 1951), 115–17.

23. Lewis, *The Voyage of the Dawn Treader*, 157.

24. Lewis, *Prince Caspian*, 118–19.

25. C. S. Lewis, *Perelandra* (London: Pan Books, 1983), 107.

26. Ibid., 125–27.

27. Ibid., 106.

28. C. S. Lewis, *That Hideous Strength* (New York: Collier, 1965), 381.

29. Ibid., 316.

Part 2: The Keeper of Meaning

1. Lewis, *That Hideous Strength*, 64.

2. Oswald Chambers, *My Utmost for His Highest* (1935; reprint, Uhrichsville, Ohio: Barbour and Company, 1993), Reading for December 15.

3. George Reid, ed., *The Wind from the Stars: Through the Year with George MacDonald* (London: HarperCollins Religious, n.d.), 294.

4. Lewis, *The Last Battle*, 140–44.

5. von Hildebrand, *Feminism and Femininity*.

6. *Upstairs Downstairs*, produced by John Hawkesworth, The Third Season, Volume 6, 102 minutes, copyright 1973 London Weekend Television Ltd., 1998 A&E Television Networks, videocassette.

7. Josef Pieper, *A Brief Reader on the Virtues of the Human Heart* (San Francisco: Ignatius Press, 1991), 10.

8. Ibid., 20.

9. Reid, *The Wind from the Stars*, 248.

10. J. E. Austen-Leigh, *A Memoir of Jane Austen*, 1870, included in Jane Austen, *Persuasion* (1818; reprint, London: Penguin, 1965), 338, 387.

11. Ibid., 354.

12. Ibid., 370.

13. Louisa May Alcott, *Little Women* (1868; reprint, New York: Grosset and Dunlap, 1947), 487.

14. Jane Austen, *Persuasion* (1818; reprint, New York: Penguin, 1965), 85.

15. Ibid., 103–4.

16. Ibid., 113.

17. Ibid., 185.

18. Ibid., 195.

19. Isak Dinesen, *Babette's Feast* (New York: Vintage Books, 1988), 40–41.

20. L. N. Tolstoy, *Anna Karenin*, trans. Rosemary Edmonds (1877; reprint, London: Penguin Books, 1978), 852–53.

21. Ibid., 233.

22. Mary Riso, "Perception and Obedience in Tolstoy: The Path to Infinite Meaning in a Finite World," *Studies in Formative Spirituality*, 11, no. 1 (February 1990): 61–62.

23. Tolstoy, *Anna Karenin*, 299–300.

24. Ibid., 588.

25. Ibid., 421.

26. Ibid., 818.

27. Ibid., 471.

28. Ibid., 433.

29. Ibid., 818–19.

30. Ibid., 588–89.

31. Ibid., 520, 521–22, 524.

32. Tolstoy, *The Death of Ivan Ilych and Other Stories* (1886; reprint, New York: New American Library, A Signet Classic, 1960), 155–56.

33. Tolstoy, *Anna Karenin*, 523.

34. Edith Nesbit, *The Railway Children* (1906; reprint, Harmondsworth, Middlesex, England: Puffin Books, 1960), 221.

35. William Blake, *The Everlasting Gospel* (written c. 1818), sec. 4, 1.1.

36. Msgr. Jeremiah F. Kenney, *Trust Jesus* (Baltimore, Md.: Cathedral Foundation Press, n.d.).

37. Nesbit, *The Railway Children*, 74.

38. Ibid., 131.

39. Ibid., 55.

40. Ibid., 21.

41. Ibid., 217.

42. Ibid., 112–13.

43. Ibid., 95.

44. Ibid., 179.

45. Ibid., 88.

46. Ibid., 73.

47. Ibid., 227.

48. Ibid., 114–15.

49. Malcolm Muggeridge, *Chronicles of Wasted Time, Vol 1: The Green Stick* (New York: Morrow, 1973), 18.

Part 3: The Woman of Courage

1. Josef Pieper, *A Brief Reader on the Virtues of the Human Heart*, 30.
2. Ibid., 26.
3. Josef Pieper, *The Four Cardinal Virtues* (Notre Dame, Ind.: University of Notre Dame Press, 1996), 126–27.
4. J. R. R. Tolkien, *The Fellowship of the Ring* (New York: Ballantine, 1965), 76, 87.
5. George MacDonald, *Phantastes* (1858; reprint, Grand Rapids: Eerdmans, 1981), 159.
6. Jane Austen, *Pride and Prejudice* (1813; reprint, New York: The Modern Library Edition, 1995), 9.
7. Ibid., 67.
8. Ibid., 79.
9. Ibid., 253.
10. Ibid., 99.
11. Ibid., 151.
12. Charles Dickens, *The Personal History of David Copperfield* (1849–50; reprint, Oxford, England: Oxford University Press, 1994), 58–59.
13. Ibid., 61–62.
14. M. Scott Peck, *People of the Lie* (New York: Touchstone Books, 1985), 123–24.
15. Dickens, *David Copperfield*, 132.
16. Ibid., 47.
17. Peter Ackroyd, *Dickens* (London: Sinclair-Stevenson, 1990), 6.
18. Dickens, *David Copperfield*, 131.
19. Ibid., 211.
20. Ibid., 212–14.
21. Ibid., 224.
22. George MacDonald, *At the Back of the North Wind* (New York: Morrow, Inc., 1919), 70.

23. Charles Williams, *Descent into Hell* (1937; reprint, Grand Rapids: Eerdmans, 1949), 17.
24. Ibid., 96.
25. Ibid., 57.
26. Ibid., 98.
27. Ibid., 98.
28. Ibid., 101.
29. Ibid., 169–70.
30. Ibid., 101.
31. Ibid., 122, 124.
32. Ibid., 162.
33. Ibid., 170–71.
34. Ibid., 108–10.
35. Ibid., 109.
36. Ibid., 112.
37. Ibid., 208–9.
38. C. S. Lewis, editor, *Essays Presented to Charles Williams* (Grand Rapids: Eerdmans, 1966), x.
39. Ibid., xiii.

Part 4: The Wise Woman

1. Leanne Payne, *Listening Prayer* (Grand Rapids: Baker, A Hamewith Book, 1994), 84–85.
2. C. S. Lewis, *Till We Have Faces* (1956; reprint, New York: A Harvest/HBJ Book, 1980), 75–76.
3. Ibid., 22.
4. Ibid., 173.
5. Ibid., 307–8.
6. Ibid., 308.
7. Evelyn Waugh, *Brideshead Revisited* (1945; reprint, Harmondsworth, Middlesex, England: Penguin Books, 1962), 387.
8. T. S. Eliot, *The Cocktail Party* [1950] in *The Complete Poems and Plays 1909–1950* (New York: Harcourt Brace & World, 1971), 364.
9. Ibid., 361.
10. Ibid., 359–62.
11. Ibid., 363.
12. Ibid., 364.
13. Ibid., 357.
14. Ibid., 364–65.